This picture was taken at Connelly Springs, North Carolina in 1891. Note the large "cow catcher" and tall smoke stack.

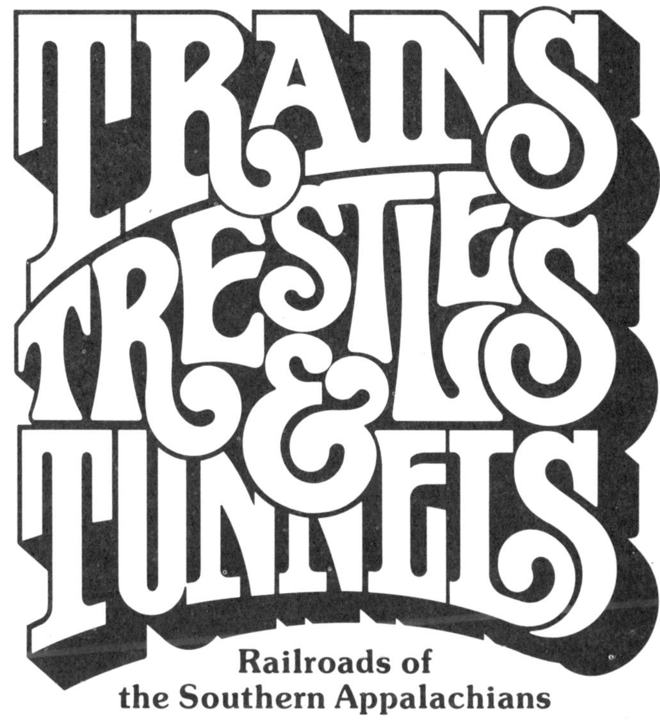

Railroads of the Southern Appalachians

by Lou Harshaw

Published By

Asheville Chapter
National Railway Historical Society, Inc.

Library of Congress No. 77-77409

Book Design by Kelso Associates, Ltd., of Asheville

Published by

Asheville Chapter
National Railway Historical Society, Inc.
Post Office Box 153
Asheville, North Carolina 28802

First Printing 1977

Hexagon Company
Asheville, North Carolina

Second Printing 1980

Copple House Books
Lakemont, Georgia

Third Printing 1989

Asheville Chapter, NRHS
Asheville, North Carolina

This edition printed by
The Hickory Printing Group
Asheville, North Carolina

Color Photographs

Front Cover, Back Cover and Photos 1, 3, 6, 7, 8, 10, 12, 14, 15, 16 by Lou Harshaw

Photos 5, 11, 13, by Kyle Morgan

Photos 2, 4, 9 by Ewart M. Ball III

Black and White Photographs

Pages 11 (left), 15, 25, 59, 63, 64, 65, 67, 71, 72, 79 by Kyle Morgan

Pages 7, 9 from Kyle Morgan Collection

Page 53 by Ewart M. Ball III

Title page, pages 49, 73, 83, 89 courtesy of United States Forest Service, National Forests in North Carolina

Pages 16, 39, 51, 52 courtesy of Graham County Railroad

Pages 5, 8, 17, 18, 21 courtesy of Southern Railway System

Pages 10, 13, 24, 28, 29, 30, 33, 34, 35, 37, 40, 68, 80, 84, 87 courtesy of Pack Memorial Library, North Carolina Room

Page 61 courtesy of Biltmore House

Page 77 courtesy of Tweetsie Railroad

Pages 11 (right), 19, 20, 23, 57 by Lou Harshaw

Art Drawings

Pages 75 (top and bottom), 81 by Dr. Robert S. Jones

ISBN 0-9623532-0-5

This book
is dedicated to
my son, Richard

Opposite page: Southern steam power labors up the
4.7 per cent grade of Saluda.

CONTENTS

WESTERN NORTH CAROLINA RAILROAD

Early on, when this was a young country just aborning and its eager, restless people were pushing westward from the coastlands, they soon encountered the formidable fortress of the Great Southern Appalachian Mountain Range. From the pleasant rolling piedmont the blue and purple giants rose in the distance, brooding, silent, mist shrouded, rugged, dangerous and most of all difficult to travel.

A footpath into the hills became a wagon road and for many years the old Buncombe Turnpike was the only entrance.
Down this well-worn route from the heart of the Blue Ridge to the populous regions of the low country came the hog and turkey drovers, the hearty mountain settlers who on foot brought their livestock to the markets in the flatlands.

As the years passed, the settlers, mostly "loners" seeking the freedom and solitude of the rough, locked-in land, penetrated the last stronghold of the once widespread and powerful Cherokee Nation. With them, came the stage coaches. They traveled over the Turnpike from central South Carolina northward and westward. The old Federal Road came up from Central North Georgia nearly to the North Carolina line and on into the East Tennessee area. A lot of this "traffic" swung northeast from this well-traveled route. Way stations sprung up and the drovers and the stages had a place to stop, eat a meal, rest their passengers and their stock, sleep a night and then move on.

Asheville was yet a tiny village when the first idea of a railroad into the mountains was advanced.

Swannanoa, near the crest of the sharp fall-off of the mountains, was only a stop over with maybe a rude and rough lodge for refreshment of foot and stage travelers.

In the years just prior to the Civil War, the westward boundaries of the State had firmed up. Most of the present-day delineations of the counties had settled in place, but it was plainly evident to state and regional leaders that if North Carolina was to benefit from the social and economic development of the remote areas of the western section of the state, then transportation to and from the mountains must be made easier, quicker, and safer.

Railroads, then expanding rapidly all over the country, particularly in the north, had to be the answer.

So, in those uneasy and quarrelsome times before the war, a group of men came together in the Piedmont to conceive and endeavor to construct what was called the North Carolina Railroad. Little did they know what was a long and arduous task they had undertaken and how many years would pass before it would at last be completed. Neither would they know the names of the many who would perish in the labor or those who finally were to oversee the completion. For many trials and tribulations were to beset both labor and management in this monumental undertaking.

It was in the 1848-49 session of the North Carolina State Legislature that John Motley Morehead, a widely known business and civic leader of the times brought forth the bill to charter the North Carolina Railway. It was he who was to push for the charter until it finally passed and then to become the first president of the railroad. His motto then became: "The Road must be built . . ."

One of the unsung heroes of the North Carolina Railroad was North Carolina House of Representative Member, Calvin Graves of Caswell County, a Democrat serving at the time of the vote on the charter. A capital stock of $3,000,000, was proposed, of which the state was to subscribe two thirds. The feeling was high and the vote close. On the third reading came a tie which threw the deciding vote to Graves.

With the Democrats against it, Graves voted for the bill and it cost him his political career. His party was never to forgive him, and he was never again to hold public office. (On April 15, 1950, a bronze tablet was unveiled in his honor, at the newly built Southern Railway Station in Raleigh, North Carolina with officials of the state and the railroad in attendance.)

The men who spearheaded this construction were brilliant in their concepts of engineering, bold and highly innovative. Their basic routes and methods have remained the same until the present day and we still marvel at the engineering feats which brought the "iron" over impassable grades and, today, stand as perhaps the boldest of early railroad engineering in the country. These rail passages were accomplished under the most difficult of circumstances and suffered untold setbacks and delays. It was the day of human labor, where the backs of men and the strength of mules were responsible for moving huge masses of dirt and stone, and the building of high bridges. It was railroad men in the Blue Ridge Mountains who first perfected the technique of "development". It was the day of convict labor, of the pick and shovel, hand drilling and black powder.

In the year 1852, the first survey of the North Carolina Railroad over the mountains was made. In the two preceding years, the North Carolina Legislature had pledged financial aid for construction. Money to pay for the survey was to come from the sale of "Cherokee lands".

Scene of the warehouse train area of the "Great Flood" of 1916.

Walter Gwynn, a highly-thought-of man, was chosen to make the reconnaissance and survey the lands. Gwynn had much experience in the locating of railroads and much experience in engineering. His assistant was James C. Turner. Gwynn reported on four routes and the one from Old Fort to Ridgecrest through Swannanoa Gap and on to Asheville was chosen as being most favorable for all purposes. The route crossed the Blue Ridge and presented a very serious problem of steep grades and sharp curves and numerous tunnels. At Swannonoa Gap (Ridgecrest), the descent easterly is 1100 feet vertical in three miles, if taken directly, which is seven feet in 100 feet, an incredible grade for a railroad. This was overcome by "development", which means the use of a long, curving, turning line around the mountainsides and sometimes looping back upon itself to secure enough distance to maintain a certain grade.

But this was the planning stage.

Construction was started in 1856 with Turner as chief engineer. In August 1857, 19 miles from Salisbury to Statesville was ready for the rails and six additional miles to the Catawba were graded. By October 1, 1858, trains were running over this part of the track.

Before the tracks could be extended further, the bitter, raging battles of the Civil War abruptly put an end to all construction.

In this, the first "railroad war", the steel rails were vital when it came to the fast movement of troops, food and equipment, and since there were many Union sympathizers in this part of the country, much destruction was done. When the fire of battle died down, most of the railroads lay in ruins, tracks torn loose, engines and cars wrecked beyond repair, equipment stolen, station houses burned to the ground.

When the two opposing armies had sorted themselves out and gone home, the ravaged South began to put itself together with one of the first things being to get the railroads moving. But the devastated land served to invite many unscrupulous opportunists from the North. They were soon joined by some of the unsavory natives, and the robbing and looting operations became known as "carpetbagging" (named for the large luggage pieces carried by the incoming Northerners).

Enter then, Swepson and Littlefield.

The original conception of the North Carolina Railroad was to be an east-west system, with west to be from Salisbury into and through Western North Carolina to the Tennessee line at an undetermined point, the rest to be in the eastern part of the state. In the post war reorganization, the western section was designated officially the Western North Carolina Railroad.

George W. Swepson and Milton S. Littlefield were, we suppose, members of the carpetbagging crowd.

Swepson, a native of the state and until that time well thought of, was made president of the western division of the railroad and Littlefield, from Maine, became his partner as second in command.

In a scandal that had far-reaching ramifications even to the impeachment of the Governor, Swepson and Littlefield looted the railroad company.

It was a strange and forboding tale that was related in later years by the young engineer Pitt Terrell. He was ordered on a cold night in January of 1869, as he told the story, by George Swepson to have an engine at full steam at a certain junction near Raleigh. He was to be ready to run shortly after midnight, the darkest part of the night. The year was 1868, in the blackest days of

Opposite page: A diamond stacked woodburner crosses Gashes Creek Trestle about eight miles east of Asheville on the Western North Carolina Railroad. (Note trestle-tree trunks with bark left on.)

Two of the early engines serving the Brevard-Toxaway Inn area sit abandoned on a side track.

Reconstruction, and the frightened 18-year-old youth dared not disobey from such a high order. As he eased the engine into place a group of men came near and one of them in a long dark cloak pulled close about his face, boarded the cab. The voices swirled around in the darkness for a moment. Terrell tried to see who was in the cab and hear what was being said. He didn't succeed in either effort. The president's voice barked an order for him to make the 50 mile run to Haw River. With a $2 tip and a threat of violence if he talked, the huddled group stood by as he eased out of the yard. Building steam, he barked an order to his fireman and eased the big powerful engine to full throttle. No lights were shown, no signals given. In later years he voiced his opinion that the cloaked figure was Littlefield, who was under indictment at the time and was never seen around Raleigh again. Nor was $4,000,000 in railroad bonds which had been issued by the State of North Carolina.

But Terrell could not and would not ever say for sure that it was Littlefield — not for sure.

Judge A. S. Merrimon of Asheville was employed to apprehend and prosecute Swepson and Littlefield. In a chase that we imagine was as exciting as a modern detective mystery, Merrimon traveled to Baltimore, New York, and then on to London. For a period of more than two years he pursued them, all to no avail. Rumors later had the two, both together and apart, in various exotic and distant cities of the world.

The Western North Carolina line was in financial ruin for the second time. The road was completed and in use to Old Fort with the high mountains yet to be tackled.

Opposite page: The Perley-Crockett Lumber Company passenger train to the top of Mount Mitchell.

Left: One of the powerful Southern locomotives on the main line near Brevard in the heyday of steam.

Right: A Southern freight train takes off, down over the mountain from Saluda.

Work languished from 1872 to 1875. Then, early that year the State purchased the Western North Carolina Railroad for $875,000 and operated it for 18 months. Construction on Old Fort Mountain began in earnest. It was hard and it was slow. There was snow and a biting wind in the wintertime, rain and blazing heat in the summer. Wash-outs were frequent. Tremendous amounts of dirt had to be moved, shovelful by shovelful, but the work went on. The state of North Carolina authorized prison labor to be used on the road and it is believed that this was the first time this labor force had been used in such a way. Three hundred males and sixteen females performed 80,309 days of work in one year. During that time three miles of track were laid above Old Fort.

An intense struggle of man against the mountains now began. It was 1876 and every day, every hour of labor counted. W. P. Terrell, the same young man who ran the midnight rider to Haw River, was at the throttle of the hard-pressed work engine, the small, but powerful "Salisbury". (The other work engine on the road was called the "Junaluska".) And Terrell was yet again to figure in another historic episode on the railroad.

On April 1, in 1877, Major James H. Wilson had been elected by the Board of Directors as railroad president. Superintendent and chief engineer and it was felt by many that only Wilson with his daring concepts could direct the project to a successful completion. Even so, there were many days of doubt. Captain Jack Edwards, Confederate veteran, railroad engineer, native of Swannanoa, later recounted some of the hardships endured. After nine miles onto the mountain he recalled, the lives of over a hundred workers had been lost, the construction had cost the State of North Carolina almost a million dollars, nine miles of ties and rail had been needed to connect points separated by a distance on an air line of only 3.4 miles and by an altitude difference of 891 feet. Total curvature was 2,776.4 degrees, equivalent to almost eight full circles. On the nine miles were six tunnels — a seventh, Mud Cut, deep in the mountains had collapsed in a sea of mud and water that took weeks to dig through to become an open cut.

There was tremendous pressure. They were working against a deadline set in the construction contracts which stipulated that the engine must roll into Buncombe County by a certain date. At one time the records show that 1455 men, 403 boys, 560 carts, 50 wagons, 780 horses and mules and 44 oxen were on the mountain.

Another Confederate veteran, Captain L. S. Aldridge, a locomotive engineer working on the line, became impatient and afraid the little locomotive "Salisbury" just wouldn't have the rails to roll on by the date stipulated in the contracts. He set out to make sure the deadline would be met. Aldridge and Terrell rounded up a group of men, cut logs and began to take the heavy engine up the mountain, a rail length at a time. As the men moved the rails manually from behind the engine to the front, they, by sheer shoulder power, pushed the heavy machine forward, to again remove the rails from behind to the front. It was an agonizing race against time, but as the sun came up on the appointed day, Capt. Aldridge and young Terrell had the "Salisbury" across the Buncombe line. Terrell was to go on to serve continuously more than 30 years on the railroad.

By far the most difficult task of all was the boring of the long tunnels. Black powder was used in the blasting, the rock and dirt hauled out by man and mule. Swannanoa Tunnel, at 1,832 feet, was the longest (the others were: Lick Log, 589; Highridge, 494; Burgin, 260.5; Jarrett's, 123; and McElroy, 77). When Swannanoa was at last blasted open, the work forces meeting at precise points near the center, the date was March 11, 1879, and Major Wilson wired Governor Zebulon B. Vance the following historic message: "Daylight entered Buncombe County today through the Swannanoa Tunnel. Grade and centers met exactly." And thus ended a single project on this difficult road that had taken three years to finish, had cost $2,000,000 and taken the lives of 125 men.

The miracle of the Old Fort grade was considered completed. It had taken 27 years of determination, back-breaking toil and millions of dollars and today still stands as one of the outstanding railroad engineering feats in the country.

On April 27, 1880, the state sold the road to J. W. Best and Associates. The road was in operation from Salisbury to within about seven miles of Asheville and was to remain in this status for some years.

On October 2, 1880, the first engine, in steam, on rails arrived at Asheville. It was met by hundreds of people in great jubilation.

In due time, 1880, Col. A. B. Andrews, a great North Carolinian, and one who was responsible for building more railroads in the state than any other single man, came to be president of the Western North Carolina Railroad.

It is he for whom the Andrews Geyser, a famous fountain which can be viewed from 17 locations on the Old Fort run, was named.

Black Mountain Station in 1910.

SALUDA MOUNTAIN

From the flatland plain of upper South Carolina, Saluda Mountain rises to the sky, its upper reaches swathed in mists, a seemingly impenetrable wall of granite, massive trees, sheer cliffs, and the kind of dirt that in a heavy rain turns to a sea of mud.

For the foot-traveling pioneer, opening up a new homestead in the Appalachians, Saluda was formidable. For the stagecoach and horse-drawn wagon, it was a rocky creek-crossed roadbed. For the daring and visionary railroad men who staked the route and, later, laid the rails, Saluda was a barrier of unprecedented proportions.

But the story of the main line over Saluda began long before those work-hardened, sun-browned men entered the picture.

Perhaps it was Judge Mitchell King, a prominent South Carolinian who owned a large summer estate in Flat Rock, North Carolina, who was responsible for the beginning of interest in the construction of a railway from Central South Carolina into the mountain fastness to the north. At any rate, mostly upon his motivations a route was surveyed generally following the French Broad River Valley. There were, of course, meetings of the leaders of both states. As a result, a company was put together with its name being the Louisville, Cincinnati and Charleston (West Virginia) Railroad. But for many years it was a company in name only. One of the problems was a great controversy that arose between Robert Y. Hayne, a strong South Carolinian who supported the railroad, and John C. Calhoun, the noted politician of that state and later Vice President of the United States. Their differences were over the proper route. However, as the controversy died down the stockholders came together in Knoxville in January of 1837 and elected Hayne president. (He died at the old Eagle Hotel in Asheville two years later.)

Judge Mitchell King was then elected president. About this time a Charlestonian by the name of Joel Roberts Poinsett became interested. Being a well-known builder of roads, it was a natural project for him.

As other prominent men became associated with the proposed railroad, the North Carolina State Legislature in 1851 appropriated $12,000 for a survey from Salisbury to a point where the French Broad River crossed the Tennessee line, but neither Poinsett's interest nor the legislature funds generated action. Another company was chartered and called the Charleston, Blue Ridge and Chattanooga Railroad, but again nothing much happened. Then in 1855 a charter was issued for the French Broad Railroad Company. At this time a link was under construction from Charleston through Columbia and on to Spartanburg. (The first train arrived in Spartanburg via this line on November 25, 1859—the realization of 10 years' "hope and work".)

With the "iron" into Spartanburg, civil war broke across the land absorbing with terrible intensity the vigor, materials and lives of the people. For four long and dreadful years there was no thought except, at first, to drive out the hated Union Army and, later, to simply survive.

Thus the first phase of the long-sought-after North-South railroad

An antique steam stallion awaits a reconditioning job in the yards at Burnsville, North Carolina.

through the Blue Ridge Mountains came to a halt. After the war, other names were to become associated with the railroad, and it was to have yet another name, The Spartanburg-Asheville Railroad Company and, still later, the Asheville-Spartanburg Railroad Company. It was under this charter that the road over Saluda finally became a reality.

Dr. Robert E. Cleveland of Spartanburg was one of the main promoters. C. B. Memminger, formerly First Secretary of the Treasury of the Confederacy, the owner of a large estate and summer home at Flat Rock, was the first president of the company after the war. A local news writer of the time recalls the scene as Memminger set out by buggy, with his young son driving the horses, on the road from Flat Rock to Spartanburg to attend the ceremonies and turn the first shovel of ground that would spearhead the Herculean effort of laying rails over the mountains.

With comparative ease, the heavy hammers beat the spikes in and the rails went on the road bed from Spartanburg to Tryon. The first whistle of a scheduled train was heard in Tryon in 1877.

When the project began to bog down, Charles W. Pearson, a veteran of the Civil War, took charge of the laying of the tract and of keeping the construction moving.

The proposed route, had been from the beginning from Tryon north over Howard's Gap into what is now Polk County, North Carolina, but only 13 miles

Opposite page: Two Southern diesels bring in Shay #36, piggy back, to Topton where the line connects with Bear Creek Junction and the Graham County Railroad.

Southern Railway steam-powered passenger train climbs the steep grade into Asheville.

Early photo shows the rugged and difficult railroad construction up Old Fort Mountain. This is Point Tunnel and viaduct over Mill Creek.

in, the courageous builders were almost daunted by their tremendous task. They were also in financial difficulties. The deep cuts, proposed tunnels on this route would not only be a morale breaking slug-fest of man against the mountain but also a time-dragging, mile by mile, foot by foot struggle involving a huge expenditure of funds.

By now the railroad had another president, Col. R. Y. McAdden, reputed to be an able leader of men. Perhaps it was his bold decision to go almost "straight up" and over the face of Saluda. Here old statements conflict somewhat, but from an account in the Southern Railway records, Thomas A. Rice of Union, South Carolina, fourth son of S. M. Rice of the contracting firm of Rice and Coleman who built the road, writes:

"It was about 1876 (the Southern Railway records correct this date to read 1886) that the railroad was built from Spartanburg to Asheville. The labor was performed mostly by convicts. Money for the work was secured by county subscription and sale of bonds.

"My father, S. M. Rice, and my uncle, Col. Robert Coleman, built the road from Spartanburg to Asheville.

"The engineers were the late Col. Thad Coleman of Asheville and the late Capt. G. C. Perrin of Union. I remember that Col. Thad Coleman wanted to run the road around by Columbus Courthouse instead of going up the mountain by Melrose, but the stockholders insisted and the road was built up the now famous Saluda grade at a most increased cost. If I remember aright, it took between one and a half and two years to build the road up Saluda grade. As the contractors had to finish it by a certain time, much night work was done when

lanterns and flares were used. There were frequent landslides when men and mules were covered by falling dirt and killed."

The heavy cross-ties were cut in nearby forests. The "big cut" halfway up the mountain measures at the center more than 90 feet deep and is 16 feet wide throughout its length. The road above the town of Melrose climbs 600 feet in three profile miles and in places reaches a maximum grade of 220 feet per mile.

Saluda Mountain, in heavy use today by the Southern Railway System, carries at 4.7 percent the steepest standard-gauge, main-line railroad grade in the United States.

The first engine arrived along the completed route into Hendersonville on July 4, 1879. A contemporary newspaper clipping describes the scene as told by an unidentified eye witness:

"Suddenly the stillness of the valley was broken by the whistle of an engine somewhere down the line, whereupon there was a scurrying hither and yon. For lots and lots of people, most of whom had never seen an engine or a train, had gathered to behold the marvelous sight . . . . Every neck was craned and every eye was fixed toward the bridge over the creek where the engine would first come into view . . . . There it came! Rattling and roaring and belching a great column of smoke from the big funnel — like a smoke stack. What a monster in size it was! What a marvelous and mighty power!" (What a shame the name of this anonymous viewer does not come down to us along with the very graphic words.)

There was the "official" railroad "party" which arrived on the first train. Many speeches by officials, the mayor of the town, the president of the railroad and others. The newspapers report the speeches were "cheered and well-received"

Monument to Major James H. Wilson on the Old Fort main line. Wilson was President and Chief Engineer of the Western North Carolina Railroad.
(Note the railroad spike shape of the monument.)

Close up shows the steep Saluda grade as it starts up the mountain from Melrose. The line here connects with the safety track veering off and up the mountain.

and that the celebration, balls and receptions spread out through the fine resort hotels of Hendersonville and into Asheville.

To encourage construction on into Asheville, the voters of Buncombe County had on August 5, 1875, voted a $100,000 bond issue to the railroad, but apparently railroad officials seemed content to stop at Hendersonville. After a delay of from two to three years, the Honorable Richmond Pearson of Asheville, member of the State Legislature introduced a bill in Raleigh to revoke the railroad charter. Work on the last link was quickly begun and in 1886, the line was completed to Asheville.

In the very early days of operation, the rolling stock was a Mogul engine with 16 by 24-inch cylinders and wheels 4 feet, 6 inches in diameter. It was named "R. Y. McAdden" after the president. Another engine was named "W. H. Inman" for one of the directors; it was the regular type with 16 by 24-inch cylinders and wheels four feet in diameter. Most of the trains on the mountain were "mixed" passengers, mail and freight.

The problems of the Asheville-Spartanburg Railway line over Saluda were not to end with its completion. In the early days when steam was the power, there were many bad wrecks.

In 1880 a work train got out of control and roared headlong down the grade. At the foot of the mountain it wrecked and killed 13 workers and a foreman.

In the dawn one morning in 1894, extra engine No. 559, with 16 cars, lost its brakes and rushed down the mountain and wrecked in a tangled mass of iron, coal and timber. The engineer and fireman, a brakeman and a rock contractor all lost their lives. The conductor suffered severe injuries and 32 head of cattle were killed.

On June 17, 1890, a lead engine was helping a freight down the mountain when both locomotives got out of control and piled up near the foot of the slope. Three trainmen were killed.

In 1890, an engineer, brakeman and conductor lost their lives in a tragic accident.

The mountain was soon legendary. Though no passenger lives were lost on Saluda, it came to have a fearsome reputation and to be known and respected by every engineer and brakeman on the line.

Later, in 1889, the relatively easy construction of the mainline into Asheville was finished. Thus began the glamourous days of luxurious travel by train to the high, cool mountains and the building of large resort hotels. Parallel to this, with the completion of this period of the Western North Carolina Railroad into Asheville, began a vast expansion of trade, business enterprises, a sudden "booming" (along with most of the rest of the country, now networked with railroads) of business, particularly real estate, which didn't slow or cease until the terrible financial "crash" of 1928 which plunged the whole western part of the state into a particularly bad depression and left the city and county some 40 million dollars in debt. (A celebration was held recently which marked the entire repayment of this debt.)

But as we will note later, if the railroads helped bring on the "boom", they also assisted in stabilizing the economic recovery in later years.

One of the big Southern Railway steamers "hauling the freight" west of Graphite, North Carolina.

THE MURPHY BRANCH

With a thriving mainline out of town to the east and the route completed from Asheville south to the coastal town of Charleston, thoughts and plans turned to the route long proposed from Western North Carolina into the Midwest. Again, a daring group of railroad men assembled themselves. Col. A. B. Andrews (who was noted for his great ability in many fields) was president of the Western North Carolina Railroad, an honest and beloved man. It was he who was to lead the effort of construction to the west of Asheville, termed: "The Murphy Branch". It was to be a temporary line.

It quickly was to earn a reputation for hardship and unprecedented tragedy even in mountain railroad building. Over a terrain hardly better than experienced with Old Fort and Saluda, the work progressed slowly. In fact it was to be 1891 before the Murphy Branch was completed.

It will be remembered that at this time the Western North Carolina Railroad was owned by J. W. Best and associates. Part of their agreement upon purchase from the State was the completion of the road to the Tennessee State line and to finish construction of the Murphy branch.

Again, convict labor was authorized by the State Legislature and this led to one of the most horrible tragedies in the history of railroad construction.

The work crews had progressed to Cowee Tunnel between Dillsboro and Bryson City. A cold wind was up that day and was knife-edged blowing off the Tuckaseegee River. A careless guard shoved off a flat boat with 20 prisoners chained together, to cross on the rough waters to the opposite bank where the camp was located. As the boat tipped on one end, the frightened men rushed to the other, causing it to capsize. The terrified men clutched at each other as they sank into the rushing river water.

Only one, the "Trusty" was saved. The rest were found in a hopelessly tangled bundle of bodies on the river bottom. The one prisoner who was able to save himself, the only one not in chains, also saved the guard. His heroic deed was ruined, however, when it was discovered that he had stolen $30 from the pocket of the unconscious man.

It was as if the drowning cast a pall over Cowee Tunnel. Down through the years there have been a dozen near accidents and a number of slides to plague railroad men on this run.

The line into Paint Rock had been meant to be the branch line and with its completion in 1882, it was joined by a main line from the East Tennessee, Virginia and Georgia Railroad Company the next year. Traffic started flowing to the west and it then became doubtful whether the line on into Murphy would ever be completed. There were, however, stipulations in the contracts and public sentiment was strong for the line. Slowly the work progressed until it was completed in 1890.

"The Murphy", as it quickly came to be called, rapidly became a major carrier, at first, of the ever-increasing tourist trade from the Alabama-Georgia lowlands to the cool and popular "Land of the Sky". Later, as the tourists began to favor automobiles and the scenic motor roads north, the trains through Murphy began to carry heavy loads of lumber from the logging operations that were springing up on the slopes of the Snow Bird Mountains, the Nantahalas and the Great Smokies.

One of the last major railroad building projects took place on the Murphy Branch. The Tennessee Valley Authority undertook in 1943 to move Southern Railway tracks away from the existing route which was to be covered by waters from the huge Fontana Dam being built on the Little Tennessee River in the Great

The Murphy Branch Line runs in close proximity with highway # 19 and the Nantahala River.

Smoky Mountains of North Carolina. The finished new road is around 15 miles long and the right of way was blasted through solid rock for most of the way.

Lee Ragsdale of Knoxville was superintendent of constructiuon and he employed several hundred men on the job from September until October of 1943. (This will give an idea of how improved machinery could cut the time in railroad building, even in the most difficult terrain.) One of the unusual tasks of the operation was the removal of hundreds of graves under the supervision of E. M. Barnes of Gatlinburg, Tennessee who interviewed any number of families and relatives to secure new burial sites in other graveyards of their choice.

There are two large trestles, one 791 feet long with piers 179 feet high and the other, a structure that crosses the upper reaches of Fontana Lake.

One of the stations along the new route has been named Chikalili, in honor of a Cherokee Indian who served the railroad in that section for many years.

With the big, powerful engines moving from the east on Old Fort Mountain, the fancy gentry high-rolling in from the south on Saluda and freight and passengers traveling a daily schedule into the Midwest, the stranglehold of

A mighty Southern workhorse takes on **coal** *in the Asheville yards.*

the rugged Southern Appalachians was finally broken. The trains were to carry many products from the hills and in turn bring in both people and materials. Prosperity had, at last come to the remote Southern Highlands.

J. W. Best and Associates, having completed the Paint Rock and Murphy lines, and thus fulfilling their contracted obligations to the State, continued to operate the road for a few years, then transferred all stock, bonds, assets and liabilities into the hands of the Richmond and Danville Railroad Company. In 1905, the growing Southern Railway System formally took over what had been the Western North Carolina line, and with this, the glorious, plush and high-profit age of railroading began in and to the Southern Appalachians.

This was an era in this country that was to see the men of the so called, "Robber Baron" class all emerge and grow to an amount of individual wealth, power and influence never seen in private enterprise in the world before.

It was the magnificent age of railroading in America. That it coincided with or was a part of, the tremendous industrial revolution and the quickly expanding knowledge of mechanics taking place at that time, resulted in perhaps, the most rapid advancement of technical progress the world has ever known in a like period of time.

A Southern Railway diesel heads into the mountains near Knoxville, Tennessee.

THE SOUTHERN RAILWAY SYSTEM

For the story of the illustrious Southern Railway System, in its service to the South and more particularly the Southern Appalachians, it is only fitting that we go back to the early hours of Christmas morning in 1830. The main character in our drama is a tiny woodburning locomotive. The scene is Charleston, South Carolina and the name of the engine is appropriately the "Best Friend of Charleston". When the "Best Friend" clackity-clacked out on the rails on what was to become a 136-mile line between Charleston and Hamburg, it was not only the longest railroad in the world, but the first inaugurated regularly-scheduled steam railroad service in America. The brave and daring first passengers gasped in the the billowing smoke, clung to hand rails as the train picked up speed, and as the bulletin, "The Story of Southern Railway System" puts it: ". . . flew on the wings of the wind at the speed of fifteen to twenty-five miles per hour, annihilating time and space and leaving all the world behind." So we begin also, the Age of Speed in America which was to emerge later into the Age of Space. The significance of the little locomotive and its first trip? It was later to become a main line for Southern.

At the turn of the century, railroads in the South were a network of tangled lines, operating mostly in a haphazard manner, some of the rolling stock was excellent and efficiently managed, equipment on other lines was antiquated, slow, and badly scheduled. As we have said, the Western North Carolina Railroad had been absorbed into the Richmond and Danville line, a railroad that had been reaching out and absorbing other lesser railroad companies. The Richmond and Danville in its expansion, encountered financial difficulties and it had to be put on the market for sale. When it was purchased by a group of forward-looking men, they reorganized it on June 18, 1894 into the Southern Railway Company (later to become "System"). The charter was under a special act of the Virginia Legislature, passed on February 20 of that year. It was in 1905 that Southern formally began to operate the Western North Carolina route from Salisbury to Asheville and beyond. The Saluda route, which had also earlier been taken over by Richmond and Danville was absorbed by Southern.

The rapidly growing Southern began a long-range plan of unification, expansion and the purchase of up-to-date equipment. The largest of the lines controlled by Southern are: The Central of Georgia Railway Company, the Cincinnati, New Orleans and Texas Pacific Railway Company, the Alabama Great Southern Railway Company, and the Georgia Southern and Florida Railway Company. These, combined with a number of important smaller companies complete a system that crisscrosses most of the territory south of the Potomac and Ohio Rivers, and east of the Mississippi. A line from Louisville, Kentucky, extends across Indiana and Illinois to the Mississippi at St. Louis, Missouri. Northern posts are Washington, D.C., Cincinnati and Louisville; to the west St Louis and Memphis. Port cities are Norfolk, Morehead City, Charleston, Savannah, Brunswick and Jacksonville on the Atlantic Coast and on the Gulf of Mexico, Mobile and New Orleans.

Down through the years, Southern Railway, as it has to a much larger degree in the entire Southern region, has contributed mightily to Western North Carolina. It united the area with the rest of the state and opened the doors to the country, was one of the major large employers, investors, and tax-paying industries of the region. With its slogan, "Southern

Serves the South", its economic impact was tremendous.

Southern has had its share of famous trains. The "Carolina Special" ran from Charleston, South Carolina, to Cincinnati, Ohio. The sleek and fleet "Southern Crescent" was a glamorous link between Washington and New Orleans. Legendary figures like Casey Jones and John Henry were born out of the beginnings of railroading in Southern's territory. It was the first major railroad to convert totally to the new and controversial diesels. Today Southern cars are to be seen shuffling in and out of the railyards of almost every major city in the United States. Southern made its mark in the mountains: It set out to make absolutely certain that there would be no more life-taking, train-wrecking pile-ups on Saluda and at great cost, constructed two long sidings that end in a counter-movement, uphill grade, gradually slowing the trains to a stop. They instituted the strictest of operational procedures on Saluda.

One of the old timers who worked for Southern during the days of steam gives us in his own words a description of how the trains were handled moving over Saluda:

"The mileage from Biltmore, N. C. to Spartanburg is measured from Biltmore. Saluda is 31.9 miles from Asheville (Saluda is at the top of mountain). Melrose is 35.0 miles from Asheville. Melrose is at the bottom of mountain. This would make the distance between Saluda and Melrose 3.1 miles. Due to the steep grade resulting in many run aways, accidents and deaths, two safety tracks were constructed. Safety track No. 1 was located half way down the mountain. A switch tender was on duty 24 hours a day. The safety tracks were constructed to lead off from the main line up the side of the mountain. The switch was always set for the train to go up into the safety track, however, if the train descending the mountain was under proper control, the Engineer would blow the whistle and the switch tender would throw the switch to the main line and permit the train to proceed down the mountain. Safety track #2 was located at Melrose, the bottom of the mountain with the same method being used. When the Diesel locomotives replaced the steam locomotives, safety track #1 was removed, however #2 is still there."

The power and improved ability of the modern diesels have virtually eliminated accidents on this steepest of railroad grades.

It was in 1916 that Southern, in Western North Carolina, suffered the greatest tragedy in its history and only by the sheer courage of its gallant men was it able to rebuild and carry on. Early in July of that year, rains began in the eastern part of the state. Blowing westward in ever-increasing torrential downpour, by July 14, they were sweeping up and over the Blue Ridge, pouring an unprecedented intensity of water out of the dark and stormy clouds, flooding the headwaters of the many mountain rivers and streams. The railroads, clinging tenuously to the mountain sides, following the low levels of the river banks were highly susceptible to floods. The high wooden trestles in their complicated cross-log pattern and the geological make-up of the rocky soil had a tendency for massive slides. Almost within hours, the roaring waters rushed down the French Broad into the trainyards by the river at Asheville. All manner of debris was swept on by the waters — houses, trees, cars and unbelieveably heavy locomotives went with the floodtide. (As told in the Graham County Railroad story one of their big engines went down the river and has never been found.) The low-lying town of Biltmore was devastated. The waters rose so rapidly, cars were left in the streets as people ran for higher ground.

The water continued to rise and destroy on the 15th. On July 16th, the waters of what will always be called the "Great Flood" reached their peak and in the dusk of that evening the rains began to let up, the waters to crest and then, slowly, to recede. By early next morning, the townspeople began to assess the damage.

The beautiful and popular Riverside Park, a recreational area of many acres, had been completely washed out. Warehouse owners in the storage and service district of the city had to bail out tons of goods at a loss of thousands of dollars and repair damages to buildings at a cost of more thousands. The personal loss was great and some lives had been taken. Hundreds had lost cars, suffered great damage to their houses, farms and livestock. But the railroads, by far, had taken the brunt of the havoc of the churning black waters. The tracks and rolling stock in the Asheville yards would have to be dug out from the tons of mud and debris, there were derailed cars, broken and scattered equipment, much of it completely covered in the drift. But if the Asheville yards were bad, out on Saluda, it was almost hopeless devastation. Just getting the work crews out on the tracks was an extremely difficult task. Mud was waist deep in places, rails were off down the mountains and all the time, on the still-soaking terrain, there was the fear of the slides that could bury and kill within minutes passing. Above Old Fort and in the rugged mountains of the Clinchfield, the damage was just as bad.

For 38 days, with all crews on emergency duty laboring from sun-up to sun-down, the clearing and repair went on. In the meantime, to the west, on the Murphy and Paint Rock branches, the damage had not been as severe and it was this that saved the railroads. The trains were able to move out over these lines carrying freight and passengers. The first passenger and freight ran on the temporarily repaired line on August 3, but it was to be much longer before the lines were put in good repair and restored to their "permanent" condition.

So, after the heart-breaking devastation of the "Great Flood", Southern began to recover, and spread over the South. If we natives did, down through the years, pass an occasional joke about "a slow freight through Georgia" or if those rapid-express engineers in the north, flying flat out over the western wheatfields, or roaring into the cavernous depths of the vast and new Cincinnati train station or Grand Central in New York, tended to look down their noses at the legendary Southern double header, pulling a hundred cars at a crawl up the steep Saluda Mountain, then we really didn't mind. We knew Southern was "our" railroad and it gave good service. Of course, as the "auto" became the mode of travel, as good highways began to fan out over the South, passenger service began to decline. But Southern continued to develop its freight

Howland Railroad which ran through the area now covered by Beaver Lake in Asheville.

business and to keep ahead on new equipment. The train yards were equipped with computers and other electronic devices. As the big manufacturing plants moved to the circle of sun in the South with its available labor, raw materials and highly livable climate, Southern grew and expanded its freight business. While the "big" railroads in other parts of the country fell into a decline Southern put on new diesels and added more freight cars.

Southern however, was suffering along with the rest of the nation's railroads, a drastic drop in passengers.

On December 5th in 1968 the famed Carolina Special moved over the rails from Oakdale, Tennessee, into Asheville, and raced on its usual schedule on into Columbia, South Carolina. The next day the train came back through on its return trip.

Four Asheville city officials, Mayor Earl Eller, Vice Mayor Frank M. Mulvaney, Councilmen J. Walter McRary and William F. Algary, on a sentimental whim, had traveled to Hot Springs where they joined the train on its run into Asheville.

It was the Carolina Special's last scheduled run.

The last regularly scheduled daily passenger train from Asheville left the tiny Biltmore Station at 9:15 a.m. Friday, August 8, in 1975 to Salisbury and returned to Asheville at 10:40 that night.

When other railroads went under and forced the U. S. Government to step in, in the form of Amtrak, The Southern Railway System, with every working day a profitable one, chose not to join, not to ask for Federal funds.

W. Graham Claytor, Jr., President, issued a statement to the press: "Southern has no plans to join Amtrak next March or at any other time."

At end of 1975, Southern had a total of 23,771 employees, a payroll of $299,054,118, was operating on 10,517 miles of road and was paying back to the states it serves a total of $32,791,236 in taxes.

On January 9, 1977, the Washington, D. C. based Southern announced that it had become the first privately owned company in the National Capitol to report over a billion dollars in revenue in one year. The Company also announced a ton-mile increase in the last ten years from 33.5 billion in 1966 to an estimated 45.6 billion in 1976, an increase of around 36 per cent.

Sulphur Springs Hotel located near a natural springs near the present Asheville School for Boys.

We have given you some of the milestones of Southern in the mountains, the proud pounding of the wheels, the excited sound of the whistle as the engines arrive for the first time at a destination of new track. We have mentioned the coming of the diesel, never as romantic, never the subject of the songsters, not the hero of the poets as the fire-breathing, heavy awesome presence of the steam locomotives. Trains were a big part of the world of Mark Twain. They dominated the world of Thomas Wolfe. Johnny Cash still dreams, talks and sings about the "high-rolling steel wheels" that takes us back to a time that will never be again. What was it about these old steel-ringing iron horses that excited us so much? There are as many answers as there are lines stretching out from a major railroad yard. Perhaps one would be because the train, as a transportaion concept was so uniquely American, so much a part of our growing up as a nation. The trains showed the ordinary citizens for the first time how big this nation was, how wide the rivers, how high the mountains, how hot the deserts. They brought us different kinds of people emigrating from every foreign country and helped us mix and mingle in the small hamlets and villages of the back country.

The trains with their catering to the rich, elite tourist trade, the resort traffic; the luxurious Pullman cars, the elegant diners endowed the railroads with a glamour not heretofore ever associated in any way with transportation. They fired the imagination and spawned a deepseated desire for motion — a wanderlust among the masses, that has stayed and grown and to this day causes us to be termed "The Restless Americans". Of course, we now travel in automobiles over broad concrete highways. In the final analysis, is this it? We believe not. It was the big, black, coal-burning engine that thrilled us. From the rhythmic, ringing chant of the work crews echoing in the hills as they pulled the heavy rails forward, a back-breaking length at a time — until the long, low whistle of the arriving train reverberated through the hills, our thoughts were of the locomotive and the men who drove her. We can look back and see that the big steam locomotives were the first mastery of massive raw power by the Americans. It began a drive within us that has never stilled, even through to the age of Air and Space.

But the steam locomotive was no push-button operation. It was cooperation between man and machine. Each one was different, and an engineer worked on the line for years before he mastered the art of driving steam. Some never mastered it. Harnessing the power of the old steam engines required consumate skill and those who could do it became folk heroes.

The railroads not only helped shape the economy of this country and in good measure helped form some of our political and social philosophies, but created within us our restless spirit, our love of adventure, our materialistic yearnings and our need to feel the surge of powerful machines around us, as good or as bad as that may be.

Opposite page: Mount Mitchell Hotel at Black Mountain.

TRAINS AND THE TOURISTS

The trains brought the first tourists. In the beginning the visitors were quite different from what they are today. For one thing, they came to stay two months instead of two days. The ladies wore long flowing dresses and carried ruffled umbrellas to ward off the sun's rays. The most casual dress for men was a heavy white cotton suit and black string tie. The most strenuous activity for ladies was an afternoon's walk through the gardens and the men were allowed to remove their coats for lawn bowling.

As the rails were laboriously extended into the hills of the Southern Appalachians and the high wooden trestles flung up between the ridges, the combination of relatively cheap and comfortable travel with the spectacularly beautiful mountains and high cool climate was irresistible. The railroads themselves, quickly realized the potential of the "summer trade". They began to actively promote it and later began to buy up land and construct hotels of their own in order to house and make money from the vacationing families. It was around 1890 that an unprecedented era of hotel building in the southern mountains began, hotels so luxurious, with such fine service and food that this was to rapidly become one of the most outstanding vacation and health areas in the east. In a recent Asheville Times article, writer Ted Carter says:

"The year 1890 was a big one for Asheville. The square had just been paved. A grand opera house had been opened on Patton Avenue. Work had begun on George Vanderbilt's Biltmore House. Bingham Military School moved to town. Street cars were operating. Public schools had been opened. The city had been lighted by electricity and it had a water works. There was a new county courthouse and there was talk of building a city hall and a city market.

"The depot at Best (Biltmore) was Asheville's front door, but the road from the east still came down from the Swannanoa Gap at Black Mountain following Christian Creek, then it rambled through Azalea, down Haw Creek, and crossed the hill to Ross Creek (where Kenilworth Lake is now), passing through Happy Valley (Chunn's Cove) then through Fontainbleau (Kenilworth Road at Normandy and Duke Streets) and Brackett Town to make a junction with Biltmore Avenue above Newton Academy (Forest Hill Drive)."

But in the early days of the stages and the drovers coming through from Tennessee, there had only been the old way stations and nothing more than a scattering of houses and stores where Asheville stands today. The first such station in the vicinity seems to have been Alexander's Inn, built about 1800 near Swannanoa. It was erected by George C. Alexander, whose father served in the state legislature in 1791 and was the first Justice of the Peace of the Buncombe County Court. It was a stage stop, a day's trip from Asheville, before beginning the rugged route down the mountain to Old Fort. The old building contained a trap door for guests to hide from the Indians. Alexander's was still functioning as an inn when, much later in the 1880's, passengers began arriving on the newly built railroad which for many years terminated in this area.

No record of early hostelry would be complete without mentioning Sherrill's Inn built in 1806 as a family residence by John Ashworth on an original North Carolina land grant.

It became a tavern when it was purchased and enlarged in 1834 by Bedford Sherrill. Sherrill was a mailcarrier from Salisbury, by way of Lincolnton and Rutherfordton into Asheville and also owned a four horse stage coach line.

Opposite page: The old Eagle Hotel. (Note stage coach.) One of Asheville's earliest hotels.

Sherrill's, as it became known, was a popular place with travelers, who were, in those days, mostly upon the road due to necessity. It was a favorite place of the drovers and had accommodations for the hogs. The rations for the animals consisted of chestnuts and corn. Sometimes one of the succulent porkers was left behind as payment for lodging, and became a fine meal on the table for the other guests. The property remained with the Sherrill family until 1904 when it was sold to J. F. Spaw. In 1916 Judge H. T. Phillips of Lexington bought it and then sold it to James G. K. McClure. The historic old Sherrill's Inn in its picturesque setting dominates the mountain upon which it sits and can be viewed from the road below as it winds upward into Hickory Nut Gap. The rambling structure with its old boxwood and other shrubbery, meandering paved walkways and sturdy stone chimneys is now occupied by McClure's daughter and her husband, the James McClure Clarkes and their children.

(Before the big building boom began, another overnight hostelry which caught the incoming turnpike travelers was the Buck Hotel built in 1825 by James M. Smith on the corner of College Street and Biltmore Avenue. Later the famous Langren Hotel, first steel girder construction in Asheville was built on this site now occupied by a three tier parking building.)

The Eagle Hotel, built in 1814 on South Main Street (now known as Biltmore Avenue) is said to have been the second hotel in Asheville. (A hostelry owned by Col. James Alexander located on South Market Street is said to be the first.) The Eagle was a very popular hotel, considered quite luxurious for its day. It enjoyed an abundance of the early carriage trade and then in 1879 when the Swannanoa Hotel was built on the opposite side of the street and, though not as large as

the Eagle, became the social center of the region, the hotels became arch rivals. A 1936 article in the Asheville Citizen describes the scene: " . . . when the railway was built as far as Biltmore, the hotel hackmen would race for guests. As they returned from Biltmore Station, old timers recall the drivers would come to town with a flourish as they rounded the curve some distance from the hotels. The hacks were drawn by four horses. The drivers had horns and the hacks and horns were splendidly rigged. Both hotels had musicians and often guests were given boisterious receptions on the porches of the hotels as they entered the lobbies."

Many things were notable about the Swannanoa, namely it had the first bathroom in this section of the country. The story goes that when George W. Pack came to Asheville for his health about 1880, he booked rooms at the Swannanoa. He informed the management that he absolutely required a bathroom and one was built in an adjoining room with a water reservoir of its own. Later, an invitation was issued by the hotel to the local gentry to come and view the new bathroom and talk was rampant in the town for months about the "bathroom reception" held at the Swannanoa. There were thousands of prominent guests at the hotel over the years and many of the old newspaper clippings mention the splendid ballroom. It was, at 3,400 feet, one of the largest in the South and many glittering balls and other affairs drew the socially elite from all over the region.

In 1905, the Swannanoa merged with the Berkley, then located on the present site of the Kress building on Patton Avenue and became even more famous as the Swannanoa-Berkley. Later, as other newer, finer hotels were constructed and drew away the cream of the social set, the Swannanoa-Berkley was sold to the Milner Hotel chain and was renamed the Milner. It later bore the names of Earle Hotel, then the Home Hotel.

In 1830, the elaborate Carrier Springs Hotel was built near the site of the present Malvern Hills development, near Asheville one of the very famous resorts built around the mineral springs of the area. These sulphur springs were discovered in 1827 by Robert Henry and his slave, then the first wooden structure was built on a hill above it. It burned in December of 1862. A new building was erected in 1867 by E. G. Carrier and was the best known of the three structures on the site. This building became the Belmont and was destroyed in September of 1891, while under the management of Dr. Carl Von Ruck. The Belmont enjoyed the first electric elevator in the South. From 1889 until 1894 an electric railroad ran a regular schedule from Asheville to the hotel carrying many well-known personages who were guests of the hotel.

Another famous inn, built for its healthful waters was the Sulphur Springs or Hot Springs Hotel, built in 1810. It was owned by the railroad and was stationed on a site on the French Broad River near the Tennessee line. In 1840 the Hot Springs burned and was replaced by the Mountain Park Hotel in 1886. Later, as the mineral water fad died, the hotel fell into financial ruin and was destroyed.

The Cherokee Inn which had an illustrious history prior to the Civil War stood on the site of the present First Baptist Church of Asheville. It was constructed of brick, four stories high in 1856, to be used as a dormitory of the old Asheville Female College. Its history as a hotel began in 1888 when a Mr.

Hegar bought the building and remodeled it. The venture was not prosperous for Hegar or when it was sold to a Professor H. C. Greenwell in 1899. In its first years it was known simply as The Oaks. In the ensuing years the building continued to operate as a hotel under many owners, many managers, among them the most notable and most successful, D. W. Misenheimer. In 1908, the building was sold to R. R. Robinson of Forest City, who repaired it and changed the name to Cherokee Inn, the name best remembered by historians. Later, after being sold again and used as a YWCA for a number of years, it was then purchased by the church for their present day imposing structure.

The first Glen Rock Hotel which was opened in 1890 and stood on Depot Street opposite the Southern Railway Station was, for more than 40 years, one of the finest hotels in this section. Its architecture was in the best tradition of the period with many chimneys and gables. In 1930 after many years of service the old building was torn down and the present Glen Rock building was constructed.

The beautiful old Margo Terrace must be mentioned. It was a true landmark located on the hill at the intersection of North French Broad and Haywood Street by William G. Hunt of Cincinnati in the year 1890. It took its name from its first manager Miss Margaret Gano, who operated it as a boarding house. It was closed December 11, 1928, with workmen coming in to move out the furniture just as the last guest was leaving.

One of the most tragic factors in the history of these early hotels is that most of them were destroyed by fire. One of the most spectacular conflagations ever to take place in the area was on the night of April 14, in 1909, when the large Kenilworth Inn, one of the best

Opposite page: The Fleetwood, never finished, stood for years as a giant steel skeleton atop a high mountain near Hendersonville, North Carolina.

Hot Springs Hotel, located near the present town of Hot Springs, North Carolina.

known of all the early hotels, burned to the ground. Newspaper articles in a horrifying account, tell of how the sky was "lit like noonday." Fortunately, the guests escaped, but without taking jewels or other belongings. These were lost in the leaping flames which were visible for miles.

Kenilworth was erected in 1891 by Senator Joseph M. Gazzam of Philadelphia, the only one to suffer severe injury in the fire. Other stockholders were the Southern Railway and George W. Vanderbilt. Some of the leading hotel men in the country were at one time or another associated with the Kenilworth. The construction of a new Kenilworth Inn was started by J. M. Chiles in December, 1913. It was used by the Federal Government from 1917 until 1922 as a hospital. After this it became a hotel again briefly, then in 1930, the building was acquired by Dr. William Ray Griffin and Dr. Mark A. Griffin, renamed Appalachian Hall and converted into a treatment center for nervous and mental disorders. It is still in operation today.

So, as we have said, in the period beginning around 1890, many large hotels flourished and construction was begun on many more with their chief promoter and mainstay of transportation being the railroad. Beyond a shadow of a doubt, the most renowned of these, the most noted and luxurious of all, was the first, stately Battery Park. The magnificent structure crowned a high hill to the northwest of town, first called Stoney Hill and later named Battery Porter, because a Confederate officer named Porter maintained a battery here to defend the village during the Civil War.

Before that, according to Dr. J. A. Sondley, an eminent Asheville historian among other worthy attributes, the Cherokees fought the Shawnees and the Catawbas on the battery. Here on a breezy April 5th in 1865 the citizens of the town looked down the hill northward toward the point where Broadway crosses Glenn's Creek before reaching the French Broad River and watched a detachment of Union troops being forced back by local forces in the Battle of Asheville.

Col. Frank Coxe, seeing the booming increase in visitors to the Southern Highlands in the wake of railroad building was the developer of the hotel. He purchased the hill for $16,000 and his grand new hotel opened to the public on July 12, 1886. Its broad verandas looked out over the incomparable scenery of the Swannanoa Valley and Mount Pisgah. The names of the famous guests echo in the mind: Grover Cleveland, William McKinley, William Henry Harrison, Theodore Roosevelt, and Franklin D. Roosevelt.

It was here on this same veranda that George W. Vanderbilt of the shipping and railroading family, who came for the first time in December of 1887, after having traveled over most of the world, stood and looked out over the rolling hills and the distant mountains and decided to build his home here. It is known the world over as Biltmore House.

Major James W. Wilson, engineer for the Western North Carolina Railroad, chose the site and constructed Round Knob Hotel at Andrews Geyser in 1885. One of the purposes of Round Knob, built before dining cars were put on the rails, was to furnish meals to the passengers on the main line between Old Fort and Asheville. The hotel burned in 1903.

Worthy of our particular attention, the 150-room Toxaway Inn was opened in 1903, on a sparkling mountain lake in the Sapphire Country of North Carolina. It advertised only for millionaires as guests, the most glamorous, most social of all. Seemingly, the hotel had everything — a shoreline of blue waters, 15 miles long, 30,000 acres posted years in advance for a virgin forest of hunting and fishing. There were electric lights, elevators, steam heat, a large ballroom, a billiard parlor, golf, tennis, bowling and horses. From Hendersonville up through Rosman, four trains a day came up into the green folded mountains to serve the hotel — all Pullmans. For 13 years the glittering crowd attended. There were special railroad sidings where the wealthy tycoons of the day could "park" their plush and lavishly decorated private railcars. Then in 1916 came a soggy, wet year. One damp and misty day in the spring, the guests gathered, watching as the 50 foot high earthen dam grew weaker by the hour. They sent messengers to warn the people below.

Then with a 30 foot wave, the dam broke. Dragging trees, small boats, mud and shrubbery, the angry, pent-up water crashed into the 16 mile long gorge, never abating until it flowed onto the plains of South Carolina, carrying and destroying all in its path.

The next day, the guests, who had packed their bags during the night, got on the trains and went away. They never returned. The lovely inn that had stood by the deep sparkling waters of the lake never again opened its doors to guests.

Although most of the hotels and inns built during the height of the railroad-tourist era are gone, some remain and we could go on and on: High Hampton Inn at Cashiers, the Jarrett House at Dillsboro, Nuwray Inn at Burnsville, Woodfield Inn at Hendersonville. In Asheville the New Battery Park was built by E. W. Grove who also built the fabulous and still thriving Grove Park Inn. The George Vanderbilt was built by a group of citizens in the later tourist history of the area. But one can think back to one of the glories that never quite was, the magnificent Fleetwood on a high mountain near Hendersonville, started in the frantic building boom of the early 1900s. All of us of this generation remember the Fleetwood which never got beyond a massive steel skeleton in the sky, visible for miles. The fancy bathroom fixtures strewn about the ground at the base of Fleetwood were carried off during the depression years and now grace many of the homes in the vicinity of Hendersonville. The hulking steel structure was torn down for scrap during the second World War.

One thinks of the trains, the comfortable Pullmans, the showy dining cars with their white linen and gleaming silver, the handsome carriages that met the trains, the hurrying porters, the bellboys, the welcoming and pretentious portals of the fine hotels. Most, as we have said, are gone, but one can go back to Round Knob, back to Toxaway, where if one is perceptive and will brave the overgrown forest roads, one can make out the old foundations. Through the trees, at Toxaway, the rush of the falls is to be heard. One can imagine the whisper of taffeta on a summer night, the faint, far-off sound of the dance music, and in the distance the whistle of the midnight special in from — where? Almost anywhere, bringing anyone, yesterday's rich and famous, yesterday's glamorous and social, yesterday's "beautiful people."

Black Mountain Inn at Black Mountain, North Carolina, (note fine detailing of construction and horse and buggy).

EARLY LOGGING IN THE MOUNTAINS

Note: Information in this article was prepared by William L. Nothstein, U.S. Forest Service, (Retired).

The first boards cut from the fine timber stands of Graham County were probably for home use and were cut by whipsaw pulled up and down by a man above the log, and one below.

The river drives for the lumber rich lands near Santeetlah, West Buffalo and Snowbird were begun in the eighties. Stumpage paid for virgin yellow poplar trees was 25 cents each. Only the best white pine, yellow poplar, chestnut, basswood and cherry were cut. Such trees had to be within reasonable horse or skidding distance of a navigable stream.

Splash dams were built on West Buffalo, Little Snowbird and Big Santeetlah Creeks. Logs were cut and floated down Big Snowbird during periods of naturally high water. These logs were also floated down Cheoah River and the Little Tennessee River to a sorting boom below the present Chilhowee Dam. Men followed the logs in whale boats and freed logs or beached logs with pike poles and preavis.

Samuel McFalls of Andrews was one of the splash dam builders and river drivers of the time, and was camped in what is now the parking lot of the Joyce Kilmer Forest when word came that the lumber company had decided not to cut timber on the tract.

Each log was stamped with the owner's brand before it was put into the stream. The owners collected their logs at the sorting boom and bound them into rafts. Men then guided and rode the rafts to the sawmill at Chattanooga, Tennessee. Forrest Denton, of Little Snowbird, reports that the last river drive was in 1894.

These early loggers were supplied by trains of pack horses and mules from Tennessee —

probably Loudon. Trails had to be built for these pack trains. The Belding Trail came across Citico Creek to the head of Little Slickrock, down that drainage to cross the main creek and continue through the Yellow Hammer Gap to Cheoah River at the present site of Tapoco.

The first sawmills were the up and down type powered with water. Jason Hyde operated on Atoah Creek, John Barker had one on Long Creek, and Hardy Wiggins, reports his father operated one at Sweet Gum.

The Babcock Lumber and Land Co. cut Slickrock from about 1917 to 1921. It was a standard gauge railroad operation connecting directly to the Southern Railway at the mouth of Slickrock Creek. Skidding was with Lidgerwood overhead skidders for distances up to 4,000 feet. A single trip would bring in 2,000 to 3,000 board feet of logs. Logs were bunched to cables with horses. The grading was done with a steam shovel. Hemlock was plentiful for trestles and useful for nothing else. Five Shay locomotives were put into operation.

Even for that day, some unusually large trees were cut. The largest was a four-log yellow poplar in Big Fodder Stack Cove. Its net scale was over 22,000 board feet, Doyle-Scribner Rule. Standard gauge Southern Railway flat cars were used to haul logs to the mill. The diameter of a single log took up the entire available width of a standard railroad car.

The Kitchen Lumber Company cutting on Twenty-Mile Creek, later moved to Bear Creek, Barkers Creek and Best Creek. Standard gauge railroad grades were put up these drainages. The railroad connected to the Southern Railway. The period of operation was during the twenties.

Early logging scene in the Snowbird Mountains.
(Note construction of trestle behind the engine.)

Round Knob Hotel and Andrews Geyser were located on the Western North Carolina Railroad west of Old Fort.

High lead skidders were used to bring the logs to the railroad cars. Noah Haney was the locomotive engineer. Operations had to be terminated abruptly so equipment and steel could be moved out before Calderwood Dam was built. One jackpot of logs was left on Deep Creek.

Railroad logging was discontinued after bulldozers and logging trucks were developed. Other changes included a different use for hemlock. Once it was considered fit for trestle timber and tanbark; later it was cut for pulpwood. After chestnut became too scarce or valuable for framing, hemlock logs were run through the headsaw.

The Whiting Manufacturing Company band mill, at Judson, influenced logging operations over much of eastern Graham County. This company extended narrow gauge tracks up many of the drainages from Panther Creek to Fox Branch. Wild Cove, the site of the present Fontana Village, was logged during this period of operation. Trestles or low bridges crossed Little Tennessee River. The narrow gauge logging railroads terminated at the tracks of the standard gauge Southern Railway. Loads were transferred to standard size cars and taken to the band mill. Logs were skidded to the narrow gauge by horses and oxen.

THE IRON CLOAK OF POWER

Many still remember the courage and daring of those
who brought the "high iron" over the rugged Southern
Appalachians. We find among the railroad men in
the mountains today, the same dedication, the same
tough spirit and the same enduring
romanticism.

4

5

6

7

8

9

10

11

13

14

1. The lead engine of the Yancey Railroad pulls a load of freight cars out of the yard at Micaville.

2. The tourist train at Bear Creek Junction pulls through the cut on to the rim of Nantahala Gorge in Graham County, North Carolina.

3. Engine 1925 of the Graham County Railroad as it sits in the yard today.

4. Engine 1925 heads into Bear Creek Junction during the operation of this railroad in Graham County.

5. One of the big diesels of the Alexander Railroad sits in the yard, ready to pull off for the day's work. Note the traditional "June Bug" colors.

6. Joyce Kilmer Forest in Graham County, North Carolina preserved by the loggers and other citizen's and business interests as an uncut, primeval preserve. Now under the National Forest Service.

7. Detailing of bell of old 1925 of the Graham County line.

8. Nantahala Gorge in North Carolina typical of the rugged and scenic land through which the "Murphy Branch" was constructed.

9. Howard Herd tends the firebox of Old '25 on the Graham County Railroad.

10. The "high steel wheels" sit in the shops of the Clinchfield, waiting their turn on the rails.

11. The historic little Tallulah-Yancey Caboose "always a bright spot" on the Yancey Railroad.

12. The beautifully restored Clinchfield No. 1, oldest regularly scheduled steam engine in the United States, as it comes out of Skaggs Hole Tunnel, near Elkhorn City, Kentucky.

13. Clinchfield Car 100, private quarters of General Manager Thomas D. Moore, Jr.

14. Sunrise in the formidable and forboding Southern Appalachians.

15. The town of Saluda in North Carolina. One of the hard working Southern Railway diesels heads down the 4.7 per cent grade to Melrose.

16. One of the "work horse" diesels of Alexander Railroad picks up a load of wood for the run to Statesville.

15

16

INCLINE RAILWAY

A 1933 article from the Asheville Citizen-Times tells of a logging operation in the Plott Balsam Mountains which was serviced by an incline railway, "the longest and steepest in the world."

The incline was owned by Robert Long and R. J. Snyder, lumbermen of Sylva and was used to haul wood up and down the mountain. Two skidder machines were built on the top of Yellow Face Mountain, at an altitude of 6,200 and another about halfway down on the south side. (The Blue Ridge Parkway, at the highest point on the motor road goes over the Balsams at 6,053 feet.) The incline as it climbed the mountain had a grade of 85 percent at several places. The article says of the railway: "The road goes through and over some of the most rugged mountain land in the Balsams." The route was a total of over four miles long, with two of them almost "straight up" the south side of Yellow Face, other two going down the north face.

There were 125 men involved in the Plott Balsam lumber operations owned by Long and Snyder and the incline often made as many as 10 trips a day. The logs, after they were brought down the mountain were floated out over 18 miles of flume lines on Buff Creek and North Fork into Addie where they were shipped by rail into the Canton yards, some of it going to Champion Paper and Fibre and the rest to other paper mills.

At the time of the article, more than 26,000 cords of lumber had been cut in the operations that covered the territory from Black Rock to Jones Knob in the Balsams.

Early steam engine and crew of the southern mountain area.

FIRING UP THE SHAY

It was a day of great excitement. The morning had started soft and dark and dripping as I left Asheville and headed for Bear Creek Junction near Robbinsville in the western part of North Carolina.

I had been invited by Tom Ebright, President of the Bear Creek Scenic and Graham County Railroad Company, to participate in an event that I am sure I will remember for the rest of my days.

It was the day set to bring the fifty-year-old Shay steam locomotive out of winter retirement and take it from the Bemis Lumber Company workshop at Robbinsville down the eight-mile track to Bear Creek.

This was no snap job. Before we pulled in at the Junction, late in the afternoon, I would have spent almost seven hours watching this fascinating machine being brought to life and invested with a full head of steam for the power to haul the heavy rail cars over the mountain.

I arrived at the Junction, situated on Highway 129 which turns off U.S. No. 19 North just beyond the Nantahala Gorge. The morning had turned to white, billowy clouds against a deep, blue sky. The mountains were carpeted in their luxurious spring greens.

Tom took me to the workshop in Robbinsville and I met Howard Herd, Master Mechanic, on the line, one of two men who would accomplish the feat of the day. The other was Dan Ranger, Engineer and Vice President of Bear Creek Junction, Inc., both of them young railroading men with many years of experience and training already behind them.

Bringing the Shay to life was going to be a long process, so when Howard struck the match that lit the wood fire in the firebox at 11:05 a.m., I settled down in the doorway of the cab to wait and ask what must have seemed like hundreds of questions.

Before the day was over, I was to know what purpose most of the valves, gauges, switches in engine served. At first, we watched the water level and the steam pressure gauge. Howard had to be cautious. In the process of building steam, the Shay's boiler expands a little and so it must be brought up slowly to keep from putting too much strain on the parts.

At 11:40, I asked Howard, who was feeding more scrap lumber to the firebox, what was going on. He explained that it is similar to a huge percolator, getting ready to perk coffee.

Dan arrived and the two of them go into what must be the most complicated countdown outside a missile launching. The fire is big now, and Howard continues to add scrap wood (donated by the nearby Burlington Furniture Factory for the occasion.) He occasionally feels the outside of the firebox to see if it's getting hot. It is.

At 12:30, I was in my place in the door. Dan was all over the Shay, checking and rechecking many things of many natures. Inside, I heard a distinct belch or a hiccup from the black giant. (The Shay, named for Hiram Shay the man who invented it, was developed for logging in the mountains and served its purpose well.)

The mountain monarch was gathering itself together now and all kinds of noises could be heard.

Both Dan and Howard started a highly interesting procedure. They listened to the sounds coming from the Shay. The steam pressure began to rise slowly at first and then faster. The two men turned, adjusted, and listened, then adjusted some more. This listening process went on until the big locomotive started to move.

There were sounds on top of sounds now and the steam pressure was pushing up toward a top of 190 lbs. The racket in the shop became almost deafening and black smoke poured from the smoke stack into the peaked corrugated roof of the shop where ventilators took it off.

Ed Collins of Robbinsville came on the scene. Ed is a remarkable man who spent 36 years as an engineer on the Graham County Line. He has run this engine too many times to count and it is named for him — the "Ed Collins" on the sides of the cab in gold antique lettering. If in a moral sense only, Ed owns the cab. He is to make the run with us this afternoon.

Dan began to oil the engine. This is about a forty-five minute procedure. He uses oil all over the gears generously, like other people use water for washing jobs. The Shay, No. 1925, from the year it was built, was especially dry, having been in winter retirement. Meantime, the pressure was fast approaching 190 lbs. Just as Howard and I climbed down from the cab, the safety valves opened and the noise of the escaping steam was frightening. It was 2:20 in the afternoon.

At 3:30 we were set to move out. The huge shop doors were open to the loading yards, the tracks were cleared of debris. All the workers in the shop gathered around to watch the Shay move out. Dan, somehow or other, spotted a pinhole leak in an oil line. The acetylene torch was brought up and Howard repaired the break in the pipe. We were ready to move again and a small crowd had gathered outside in the yard.

Dan eased the big machine out, generating excitement and much verbal encouragement from the crowd. We stopped long enough to give the Shay a quick steam bath. (She had previously received a coat of black paint.)

We were all aboard again, Dan looked at Ed, pointed to the throttle and asked, "Take her down, Ed?" But Ed declined, preferring to assist Howard and blow the whistle with his special tune.

We gathered a little momentum and headed for the mountain. The Shay is known for power, not speed. It proceeds steadily on its way at a top speed of 15 miles an hour. But a Shay, on the move, is still a very thrilling sight. There are a comparative few in operation in the country.

At 3:30 on the mountain, the shadows were beginning to creep into the folds of the high ridges. Dan was running, Howard was firing, Ed was assisting Howard, and I was in the way. (The cab of a locomotive is basically for two people.)

The word had spread that the Shay will move this day and the townfolk were out to watch as Old 1925 headed out for its summer work of hauling the thousands of summer visitors who would come to ride the train. The people of Robbinsville and the area waved and cheered us on our way.

The trip down was not uneventful. Dan, at the throttle, pulled to a stop at one of the Robbinsville intersections and went to the drug store to get large Cokes for all of us. The big old Shay sat, huffing and puffing rather quietly, until he came back. The people gathered around and were seemingly delighted with "their" engine on "their" railroad.

When we were underway again Ed thought I ought to be "useful" (I hadn't paid for a ticket), so he tried me at shoveling coal. The firebox doors were operated by a foot peddle, and due to the "sway of the Shay", so to speak, two shovels of coal missed the door and went all over the floor. I was relieved of this job hurriedly. Then Ed decided that at least I could learn to blow the whistle. Everybody told me to "pull it hard". I did, and it stuck fast for a moment, blasting the neighborhood and sending the nearby farm animals into panic. (When we arrived at the Station, to be greeted by Tom Ebright, he remarked to Dan, rather dryly, I thought, that a lady had called and registered a complaint for "excessive whistle blowing" frightening the cows and causing her horse to jump the fence. Nobody said anything.)

It was 6 p.m. when we pulled into Bear Creek Junction. It had been a long day and I still had the drive home to Asheville. I was dirty from coal dust, oil and grease, but I had made some delightful new friends. At the same time, I had achieved one of my life goals — to ride in the cab of an honest-to-goodness, working steam locomotive, and so, I went home tired, but elated with my day.

Opposite page: Old 1925 chugs along bringing in the daily load of freight to Robbinsville, North Carolina.

Bear Creek Junction south of Robbinsville, North Carolina.

GRAHAM COUNTY RAILROAD

The story of the Graham County Railroad in North Carolina is really the story of the old Shay Engine No. 1925.

The old records tell us how very closely interwoven were the economy of the area and the operation of the railroad company.

John B. Veach, Sr. was to say it this way in the Graham County (N.C.) Centennial Celebration book: "In 1923 and 1924 substantial acreages of timberlands were purchased by the Champion Paper and Fibre Company-Bemis Lumber Company, and Gennett Lumber Company, comprising the watersheds of Little Snowbird, Big Snowbird, West Buffalo and Santeetla. Mr. H. C. Bemis purchased the outstanding stock of the Graham County Railroad Company, renewed the charter and started construction of the railroad over the original route from Topton to Robbinsville. The arrival of the first locomotive and cars in Robbinsville in late 1925 was cause for a big celebration by the citizens of the county."

It is entirely proper that John Veach, Sr. should help tell the story. He is the grandson of H. C. Bemis who started the Bemis Lumber Company many years ago. Four generations have served the business, Mr. Veach, in addition to being the head of Bemis, was the second President of the railroad company.

Years were to pass between the days of the Great Cherokee Nation and the time of the first timberland operations in this area.

In the very early days, the Kanawha Hardwood Company had come into the Snowbird Mountains and had constructed a number of lumber mills along Snowbird Creek. The company constructed a three foot gauge railroad known as Snowbird Valley. The railroad failed, however in 1917 and the equipment and rails were sold for scrap.

But in the spring of 1923, new faces were seen in the forests of Snowbird and there was a rustle of feet along the rocky paths. These were strong men, used to the out-of-doors, faces weatherbeaten, turned to the sun. These were the lumbermen, the men who cut, rolled, snaked and floated huge logs out of the forests.

It would be these forestry people and our first environmentalists, "friends of nature" as they called themselves, who would preserve some 3800 acres of timberland in its virgin state, never to be touched by the saws of civilization and who were to dedicate the forest to Joyce Kilmer, beloved author of "Trees." The Gennett Lumber Company owned this land originally but sold out to the Forest Service for establishment of the forest, and its maintenance for the interests of the public.

The story about the railroad actually begins on February 27, 1905, the date of incorporation by a special act of the General Assembly of North Carolina of the Graham County Railroad Company. Before any work was started, a meeting was held on October 11, 1910, with a capital stock of $150,000 authorized and a campaign started to sell the stock.

The next year, with construction still lagging, F. S. Whiting and his associates in the Whiting Manufacturing Company, purchased stock and proposed an alternate route to the one from Topton through the Gap. It was felt that the great cost of construction through the Gap made a route from Fontana down the Little Tennessee along its south banks up Meadow Branch across the Gap to the Cheoah River, then up the river to Robbinsville more feasible. The board members of the company asked Whiting to do a cost study of this route. There continued to be meetings held, but apparently there was never enough money to actually start construction on either of the proposed routes.

In a revitalization of interest and a great need for the railroad to be in operation, construction was finally begun in 1924. This was after all stock had been purchased by H. C. Bemis, president of the Bemis Lumber Company. It was after the purchase of Bemis of vast acreage of lumber lands at Snowbird, a powerful Shay locomotive was purchased from the Lima Locomotive Works in Lima, Ohio. Other rolling stock was ordered for early delivery.

The Bemis Company built a logging route up Big Snowbird Creek and a line was built into the Dick Creek section, soon the track was relaid up the old Snowbird Valley line and the whole operation was renamed the Buffalo and Snowbird Railroad. Even though, this name was never used in any equipment, all costs were charged separately from the Graham County common carriers. Shortly after the narrow gauge Buffalo and Snowbird started operating, Champion Paper and Fibre Company came in and extended the line into a new operation called "Junction" under a unique arrangement Bemis operated "Junction" and handled all logging operations for Champion.

The Shay, with the number 1925, the year it was built, was big, black and powerful. It was designed for the heavy grades and the tight curves of logging work. No. 1925 was to concern itself in this work for many years, but in addition to lumbering, the Shay hauled trains of many cars up and down the mountain. It was said that from year to year, the fire hardly ever died in the firebox of '25.

A man named Ed Collins came to work on the railroad in 1928, three years after it was built. Ed and engine '25 worked together for the next 36 years. Collins tells of days of lumber hauling and nights of freight and passengers. He knows about the railroad, he knows about the mountains and the people who live there. Ed has lived in Robbinsville and worked on the railroad through both the good and the bad times. He saw it start into operation and he saw it shut down. Twice, he had seen the steam engine die, and the boilers grow cold in the yard.

C. C. Bateman, trainmaster and conductor, came to work for the Graham County Line in 1927. He was present and vividly remembers the all-day celebration that was held at the time of arrival of Engine '25. He recalls that there was plenty of barbecue, a very large crowd, games were played, and it was an all-day affair. The engine coming up and over the mountain was a show of prideful power that day.

Wilson Carpenter has also worked through two close-downs of the train. The yards, the rolling stock, the station, all were under his watchful eye and in his care during this period. An able builder, Carpenter helped build the station house, the two log cabins that now stand on the grounds of Bear Creek Junction.

J. B. Waldrop is another Graham County veteran, having worked with the railroad in the early 60's.

Doyle Brock of the Bemis Hardwood Corporation talks about the train: "The period of high activity for the Graham Line was in the late 1920's and early 30's. At one time the line served as the only main line of transportation into the county. The train hauled a great volume of a great variety of goods including household items, cloth, hardware, tools, food and many other categories. At this time we had no passenger service." Brock sees the history of the railroad through "different" eyes. He kept all the books and records for the line for many years. Through his hands passed the work sheets of the periods of profit and loss . . . the intricate detailing of a very complex business. These old ledgers and letters tell a great deal about how things were with the economy of the county at that time.

But we are ahead of our story. We must go back almost 50 years. When the Whiting Company first graded the railroad bed and made an attempt to lay tracks. Whiting, in an effort to secure rolling stock, purchased a used 90-ton Baldwin rod engine with the apt name of Junaluska, and sent it to Asheville for overhauling. While it was being repaired, raging flood, the "Great Flood" of 1916, swept through the western part of the state and washed the big engine into the French Broad River. Although many searches were made, the locomotive was never found. With the loss of its motive power, work on the railroad came to a halt.

When Bemis came to North Carolina in the Snowbird lumbering operation of the early 20's, the lumber company bought out and completed the Graham County line. Working for an interim time was a small Shay borrowed from the Bemis Mills in West Virginia, later to be cut up for scrap.

When the new 1925 arrived, it was put to work as a Graham County road engine and as the Bemis Lumber Company woods locomotive. During the day the engine hauled log trains in the mountains above Robbinsville and at night made the run down the mountain to Topton.

Essentially, 1925 was to work for Graham County Railroad Company from the day of purchase, with the exception of seven months on a short line from Andrews to Hayesville.

Engine No. 4, the third engine to serve on the Graham County line was a great working engine, a powerful four truck type Shay that was used for some years for a lumber dry kiln. Through carelessness, the crown sheet was burned beyond repair and No. 4 was cut up for scrap.

1926, the fourth engine for Graham, was a super-heated Shay similar to 1925. It belonged to the Tallassee Power Company and helped to build the Calderwood and Santeela Dams. 1925 moved to Nantahala where it was supposed to help build this dam, but later trucks were chosen for the job. Bemis Lumber Company purchased this engine, and brought it into Graham County. It proved to be a good purchase, working rather steadily for 10 to 12 years. 1926 then became a parts engine and was used to repair and recondition 1925. This Shay steamer — now stripped for the most part — still sits on a side track on the Bemis yards rusted and long overgrown with weeds.

The number plate of this engine now reads 3229. It was originally old 1926, but in the later years of the lumber operation, the plate was burned and badly damaged. The 3229 number plate came from the narrow gauge Shay operated by Bemis put up for scrap in 1942, and then resurrected to rest at the entrance of Bear Creek Junction as an attraction for the tourist line in later operations.

The fifth engine, owned and run by G. C. R. R. was a two truck Shay and was engineered by Ed Collins for a while as the main excursion locomotive. (It was the 1923 from Conasauga, Tenn.)

We have charted the details of the engines that have served Graham County Railroad because we found it interesting to dig into the old records. This is the only railroad where we were able to trace each engine and where to this day, most of them may be seen at the yard in whatever state of repair as they may be. There is one more engine, a diesel, but we will get to it in our further chronicle of this historic little shortline.

During the years from 1961 on, many different influences, developments, growth of businesses and new business opportunities were having an effect on Graham County and the surrounding areas. Snowbird had been logged by Bemis. Their scientific approach to cutting the hardwood timber encouraged quick reforestation by natural means on the mountainsides. The slopes were again green with sturdy hardwoods, hemlock and pine. A world war had been fought and won and the young men were returning with a new appreciation of their western North Carolina high country. The county had developed. James Lees Carpet Company, now a subsidiary of Burlington Industries, had come to build a new, modern plant at Robbinsville There were other influences, in nearby Swain County the tourist boom had boosted the economy for many years. The visitors began to seek out the tranquility of Graham County, the greatly varied sports and recreational opportunities available, as well as mountain scenery unsurpassed anywhere.

In mid summer of 1966 a new life and vitality was breathed into the Graham County Railroad by a three way business merger of the Graham County Railway, Bemis Lumber Company and Government Services, Inc. from Washington (the organization which operated Fontana Village Resort). An extensive railroad museum was set up, a new depot was erected and Bear Creek Junction was opened on the lower scenic route to Topton to haul passengers. This rapidly became a popular steam tourist route, a favorite of railroad buffs.

But again, one thing and another, a wreck in 1968 in which there were no fatalities but some injuries, the struggle of the freight line to secure business, the fact that the train was in a remote region away from the main line of tourist travel, all made it impossible for the train to be financially secure.

So, while the county as a whole was in a state of steady growth, things for the railroad were not so good and not so lucrative — the little Graham County line fell on hard times.

The last run under this group of operators, filmed by Columbia Broadcasting Company was made in the summer of 1970. After this, all operations ceased.

The only movement on the yard at Bear Creek was the wandering among the standing stock of the dedicated railfans who came to study and photograph the amazing Shays, the old-fashioned Pullman cars, and perhaps to walk a distance along the track where it cuts so deeply into the mountainside. At night, all was still and lonely and quiet.

But it was not to be the end, not then. In 1973 a new group was to come in, Tom Ebright from Philadelphia, Jack Clark, III, from Florida, Dan Ranger, Howard Herd and Henry Chandler from California. They aligned themselves and made yet another effort to save the little Graham County short line and make it profitable. And for a time it seemed as though they would. Ed Collins was called back to advise and encourage. Old 25 was cleaned up, fired up and given a new coat of paint. She now proudly sported the name "Ed Collins" on her side in gold lettering, in honor of the fine gentleman who had been her engineer through so many tumultuous years. J. B. Waldrop came back so did Wilson Carpenter who had continued as caretaker of the grounds over the years.

Once again the excited summer tourists gathered at the Bear Creek Junction and then again old 25 could be heard in the distance lumbering at her best speed of 10 miles an hour on the passenger run down the mountain to the observation platform near Topton.

A new diesel was purchased to help handle the freight run. Things were going well.

But seemingly Fate has a cruel trick or two when it comes to this railroad. In quick succession, the inflationary years of the early seventies began, the recession and then energy shortage, making the size of the crowds that gathered at Bear Creek smaller and smaller. The freight business did not build up to its anticipated level. Then in the morning hours of one spring day, the storm clouds began to gather with unusually dark and brooding density on the mountain. Heavy rains began falling and soon there was a wind of near hurricane proportions. During the night of March 28th, 1975, two trestles between Bear Creek Junction and Robbinsville went out. They were a total loss.

For awhile, the officers of the company struggled to secure funds to repair the bridges but to no avail. On June 29th of that year, old '25 made its last run. The next day, the diesel made the rounds to do the "clean-up" work, to haul the last freight cars down to the Southern switch yards. Then again, Ed Collins watched old '25 being staked out in the yard.

Now '25 stands silent as does the diesel that Henry used to drive. The museum cars have been stripped of their exhibits and down along Tullulah Creek, the weeds are clogging up the rails.

Passing now and then, one can sometimes see an old timer, or a serious faced youngster standing, staring at the engines, dreaming of a world now lost, of a big powerful logging locomotive bringing out the day's load of hardwood, making the night run with freight to the switchyards at Topton. You know he hears the crash of lumber in the Snowbird Mountains, the yells of the timbermen and along the sides of Nantahala Gorge, the faint and far-off whistle of old '25 coming in. The dreamer soon moves on to return to today's world and in the falling dusk, in the yard at Bear Creek, again, all is still and lonely and quiet.

Shay locomotive No. 1925 as it sits in the yard at Bear Creek Junction.

TALLULAH FALLS RAILROAD

The original concept of the Tallulah Falls Railroad was a part of that grand scheme of building known as the Blue Ridge Railroad that began around 1850. In the beginning, four companies were chartered in the four states to be traversed from Anderson, South Carolina to Knoxville, Tennessee through Rabun Gap and along the Tennessee River. The venture was ill-fated and through 50 years of the organization of companies, perhaps aptly called such names as: The Rabun Gap ShortLine Railway Company and the Missing Link Railway Company, Blue Ridge rails reached Walhalla, 34 miles from Anderson, when construction was halted by the Civil War.

This Anderson line destined never to be completed later became a part of Southern.

The Northeastern Railroad of Georgia was chartered in 1871 and construction began from Cornelia to Tallulah Falls. In 1881, the owners, the city of Athens sold the company to the Richmond and Danville Railroad and the new line was opened shortly afterwards.

For 65 years the little shortline enjoyed a period of glamour and excitement. It carried passengers to the spectacular scenic attractions and fashionable hotels in the area. There were heavy schedules in the summer months with special excursion trains arriving all the way from Atlanta.

Even so, the line did not seem to thrive financially at this time.

The original articles of sale had required that the line be extended to Clayton by April of 1886. The existing 21 miles were sold in 1886 to the Blue Ridge and Atlantic Railroad Company which operated it for five years and then went under. Sold in 1897 by court order, the Tallulah Falls Railway Company was organized to take over.

In one last effort, to revive the old Blue Ridge dream, the new company began building north. By 1904 the line was completed into Clayton. At milepost 37.4, the line crossed the roadbed of the originally proposed Blue Ridge route using the foundation of a trestle which had been built half a century before. In the next year, track reached and crossed the North Carolina line and Southern Railway, long in the financial background of the project acquired its capital stock.

Until 1905 the trains were pulled by noisy, wood burning locomotives. The flow of the tourists trade lasted up until 1910 when a large power company announced plans for a dam. When constructed, the dam destroyed much of the scenic value of the area, business at the big hotels rapidly fell off, concurrent with this, the automobile became the popular mode of travel for vacationists. One long passenger train was all that was needed on the line in those days.

June 1907 saw the rails completed into Franklin, North Carolina. The line as it was built above Clayton did not follow the old Blue Ridge route, nor was any connection ever constructed between Anderson and Tallulah Falls. Except for some short segments near Fontana and Knoxville, the dream died at Franklin. In its later years only two moments of glory came to the Railroad, the filming of two very popular motion pictures. In 1950 the railroad was used din "I'd Climb the Highest Mountain" and in 1955, Walt Disney came to Georgia to make "The Great Locomotive Chase".

Except for the time of movie making, old "T.F." as the railroad affectionately came to be called, was never profitable in its later years. In fact it went into receivership in 1923 and operated in the red until it closed.

On March 25, 1961, the Tallulah Falls made its last run. All along the route, the folks of the different communities silently gathered along the tracks. Here and there a tear was shed. For 90 years the train had been a part of their lives, carrying them to town, their goods to market, bringing back their mail. The train had suffered good and bad fortunes — as many of them had experienced in their lives. Now it was over. The roads had been built and there were the automobiles and the trucks that traveled the highways in such great numbers.

On May 4th in 1961, in a last ditch effort to save "Old T.F." a group of citizens from two counties known as the Rabun Industrial Development Company, endeavored to raise the money to pay off obligations and begin operations again. The effort was unsuccessful and the citizens company was forced to allow the Midwest Steel Company of Charleston, West Virginia to come in and cover their bid. During the latter part of 1961 and 62, the steel company took up all the track and auctioned off all properties for scrap. "Old T.F." had ceased to be.

The old A. J. Cromwell locomotive, photographed by Kyle Morgan in 1953, in the Round House at Asheville. Engine was used in the movie "The Great Locomotive Chase" on the Tallulah Falls Railroad.

RAILS TO BILTMORE HOUSE

In writing about the railroads in North Carolina, one bit of real Americana comes to light from the late 1800's.

For months, agents had been in the rural mountain country south of the city of Asheville buying up land. Rumors were flying everywhere, but this was one time in history that actual fact so far outdid any rumor that it was hard to believe. Hundreds, thousands of acres were being purchased in the name of George W. Vanderbilt, a very wealthy young man from a family of railroad tycoons in the north. He was to build a home on the land, one of the most magnificent and costly palaces ever built as a residence in the country. It was to compare with the Hearst San Simeon and the "Breakers" at Newport.

Vanderbilt had traveled the world collecting rare and valuable antiques, paintings, furniture and hangings for his home. He hired the most highly respected architects and engaged the landscape planner of New York's Central Park to transform the small connecting farms into a garden of wondrous beauty.

The question was, how to transport the heavy building materials to the site in the days of hand labor. How to bring in the loads of men who were to do the work. The grandson of the railroad man, Commodore Vanderbilt, decided to build a line directly to the site of construction from a junction south of the town. (Later a busy little railway station was to serve the town of Biltmore. This was a small fairytale village created by Vanderbilt to house the people who worked for, or were connected with the operation of this large dairy, the gardens, or the mansion.)

Most of the letter books of the supervising architect of Biltmore House, R. S. Smith, are preserved and on file at Pack Memorial Library. There are many records, and old photos of its construction on display at the mansion. These all make very interesting reading and looking. But according to William A. V. Cecil, one of the two brothers who inherited the estate (they are grandsons of the builder, the older brother is George H. V.) there is a story of a fire at, perhaps, a freight depot, on the railroad when these may have been burned.

At any rate an old map of Asheville drawn in 1892 shows the "G. W. V. R. R." and its connection with the main line and the route to the house.

The magnificent residence with its original furnishings and other objects 'd art is open to the public and the house with its landscaped gardens remains one of the most popular visitor attractions in the South.

Opposite page: Biltmore House, Asheville, North Carolina.

BLACK MOUNTAIN RAILROAD

YANCEY RAILROAD

Just as it was the rich forest lands that brought the short line railroads into other of the Southern Appalachian areas, so it was the heavy stands of Carolina Spruce that first brought rails into the massive Black Mountain Range.

It was a man named C. L. Ruffin who in 1907, built the first eight miles of the Black Mountain Railroad up from Kona, North Carolina, through the valley of South Toe River to Bowditch. The main line of South and Western (later to be the Clinchfield) had been completed through Kona. The Black Mountain was to use it as a connection to the Midwest and South. Ruffin who had been financed by Scutt-Lambert Lumber Company for $40,000 in notes and who in turn had pledged these notes to the Holston Corporation, which was to become a part of the Clinchfield holdings, ran into difficulty when the original notes defaulted.

The Holston Corporation took over all the holdings. As new timber and mineral interests opened up, construction began in 1910 to extend the line. Due to financial aid from Judge Bliss Ray, the line was extended into Burnsville. Judge Ray then sold out his interests to the Clinchfield who took over ownership and management.

In the meantime, by 1913, when the Clinchfield interests were extending the Black Mountain line on into Pensacola and to Eskota, several large lumbering operations had bought up tracts in the mountains. The Carolina Spruce Company had set up an eight foot band sawmill at Pensacola and owned 5,200 acres on the western slopes. The Brown Brothers held 13,000 acres at Eskota. They had constructed 12 miles of track to join the Black Mountain connection at Eskota and both of these companies operated Shays over their lines and the Black Mountain Railroad into Kona to the mainline of Clinchfield.

Under the ownership of the Clinchfield who chose not to change the name, the Black Mountain operated successfully. In fact, it was a part of a large "boom" in the mountains in minerals (around Spruce Pine) and lumber.

The little town of Pensacola grew and thrived and during World War I became quite a center of activity as its "industries" produced supplies and products for the war effort. The Carolina Spruce Company had brought in its own electricity and was able to supply most of the town. The valuable timber was really the keystone of the prosperity, and the town blossomed out with a fashionable ladies ready-to-wear store, groceries, seed and feed stores, and a modern drug store with soda fountain. In 1916, a movie company moved in to shoot "Then I'll Come Back To You" starring Alice Brady and Jack Sherrell. Pensacola was used for many of the scenes and many of the local people took part.

The first passenger cars had come into Pensacola in July of 1913 and one of the most pleasurable activities of the town was to ride the excursion train in and out through the mountains where it stopped at most any whim of the passengers.

During this period, with the timber being big money in the area, the Black Mountain was running four steam locomotives that had been leased from South and Western (Clinchfield). The Clinchfield No. 5 had been assigned to Black Mountain where she was renamed No. 1, given the nickname of "Dynamite" and remained the sole power on this line until she was retired in 1955. Having given already more than 40 years of service, "Dynamite" sat in the Clinchfield yards in Erwin, Tennessee until

Three mighty rollers come along side of each other. On the left is the lead engine of the Yancey Railroad. Moving at a fast clip in the center is a big Clinchfield diesel passing another Clinchfield double-header side tracked at right. Center track is Clinchfield main line at Kona.

1968. She was then rebuilt, overhauled, and renumbered Clinchfield No. 1. This tiny engine now serves as the Clinchfield excursion locomotive and on the "Santa Claus Special."

The Black Mountain No. 2, a three truck Shay, was built by Lima Locomotive Works in October of 1914 and was used as a woods engine in the logging operations. Clinchfield Number 99 was built in December of 1905. After being leased to the Black Mountain, she was renumbered No. 3, and after the retirement of "Dynamite" became the major engine. No. 3 was returned to the Clinchfield in 1956. This was the same model engine as the IC 382, the engine in which Casey Jones was killed. No. 3 later was restored and is now on exhibit at the Casey Jones Museum in Jackson, Tennessee as the Illinois Central 382.

During World War I, with the shortage of men, a little gasoline-electric engine, called the "Jitney" was used on the Black Mountain Line. This machine came from Erwin and Kingsport to provide baggage and passenger service. Steam was still the power used to haul freight.

As the mountainsides were logged off and the roads came in bringing cars, the fortunes of the little railroad began to decline. By the time the depression hit in the 30's the line was about to fold. The track between Eskota and Burnsville was removed in 1933, and as the lumber mills shut down, so did the stores. As the families moved on to find other work, the houses became empty and were torn down or burned. Pensacola as a "boom" town gradually died away until today, few of the old landmarks are left standing. Highway 197 is built over the old Black Mountain Railroad line into Pensacola.

As the years passed, the railroad continued to deteriorate with the 65 pound rails warped and ties rotting. In May of 1954, the Clinchfield petitioned for permission to abandon the remaining 12 miles of the Black Mountain and it was granted by the North Carolina Utilities Commission and the Interstate Commerce Commission.

Even though the Clinchfield was operating the Black Mountain Line at a loss, and the equipment was depreciated, the citizens of the community knew that if Black Mountain ceased to run it would be a loss of some half million dollars annually. The local people sold $70,000 in stock and paid the Clinchfield $22,000 for track, bridges and the Burnsville depot. On April 1, 1955, the Black Mountain Railroad officially ceased to exist and the new company was named the Yancey Railroad.

Bill Banks, at age 33 became the first president and also, the youngest railroad president in the United States. Banks was a native of Yancey County whose family went back several generations of Scotch-Irish ancestry who were among the original settlers of the area.

The first order of business was the purchase of a new diesel engine for $44,000. But disaster in the form of the tropical storm Agnes struck the struggling company in 1972, doing a considerable amount of damage. Even though things looked very black for the little railroad, repairs were made and it was back in business in seven weeks. At this time, one daily run was being made between Burnsville and Kona, but the freight business was hard to generate due to the competition of trucks. It was almost a day-to-day thing, financially for the railroad in the last months of 1973. The general feeling was that the line would have to close.

About this time, when things appeared to be most discouraging, a general reorganization of the board took place and E. C. Van Horn, Vice President and General Manager of Diamond Mica Company became President with Kenneth Horton, President of Liberty Lumber and Manufacturing Company, Erwin, Tennessee, and P. C. Coletta of Burnsville, a former officer of the railroad, as Vice Presidents.

In August of 1974, J. V. (Jean) Cannon was hired as the new General Manager. Cannon with the strong support of the Board, began to revitalize the railroad. Working with him were Clarence Buchanan, Engineer and Master Mechanic, Flyod Hill, Maintenance Supervisor and Conductor, and David Riddle, Trainman.

Cannon, a native of Spartanburg, South Carolina came to Yancey County with a good railroading background. He started with the Piedmont and Northern Railroad and having served there for a number of years, moved to the Seaboard Coast Line as a Trainman.

There is no question of the dedication of this man to the Yancey railroad and his efforts to "make it go" both physically and financially. He arrived to find a two-engine, run-down 13 mile operation. With an enthusiastic Board of Directors and, in fact, the entire community behind him, Cannon today has a crew of seven men and moves over 117 cars a month over the track which has been put into good repair with all the bridges replaced and made safe.

Engine No. 1, affectionately referred to by Jean Cannon as "Blackie", has been returned Alabama. Yancey No. 2, called "Puddles" because, according to Cannon, "she has the ability to get across the tracks without falling in", is a small green 50 ton engine. No. 3 is a larger, 65 ton engine that arrived in August 1976 to replace "Blackie". All the Yancey engines are diesels.

One of Cannon's innovations on the line has been the popular and colorful Toe River Rambler, an excursion train which consists of open-sided observation cars that, with the bright green and yellow engine and the Tallulah-Yancey Caboose, wanders for four hours through Appalachian countryside that varies from the small town, country store, front yard and vegetable garden scenes of Burnsville, to the high mountains and steep grades of the rugged Black Mountain Range (which includes Mount Mitchell at 6,684 feet, highest peak east of the Mississippi).

Over the years, the Black Mountain Railroad suffered two terrible wrecks which still scar the memories of some of the old-timers. The first one took place about one-half mile below "Mud Cut" on Bolens Creek.

Workmen lost control of a wood rack flat car that was being loaded and it ran head on into an oncoming train near the Jim Griffith home, injuring Bill Mumpower and burning to death, his son, Otis, who was a fireman. Bill Mumpower's grandson, also named Bill, was later compensated for the loss of his father's life.

It was on November 5, 1920, at Micaville, that Bill Dodson, a wholesale dealer for the Blanton Grocery Company was killed in a bad train wreck which injured many others. Though no one can say for sure, the most often quoted cause of this wreck was excessive speed.

One other legendary wreck was the one in which Paul Darty of Pensacola was killed. He was the Carolina Spruce Engineer and the wreck took place on Cattail Creek. As the Yancey County Common Times tells it, "Darty was a tall, handsome man in his middle twenties from Pennsylvania. He was admired by the young boys who longed to be engineers themselves, and he was also something of a ladies man. It was his determination to keep a date with Lucy Weatherspoon, the sister-in-law of the Carolina Spruce blacksmith (Arrowood) that led to Paul Darty's untimely death.

"Each engineer made two runs up the mountain each day to bring back a load of logs to the band mill. Darty had planned a meeting with Lucy for that evening, and in anticipation finished his two runs in record time and was back in Pensacola by 2 o'clock. Because he had returned so early, he was ordered to make a third run. Darty refused, but his boss ordered him to make the run. The young engineer was angry and announced, 'I'll be back by 4 o'clock or run this train into hell!' Darty left the mill in his No. Shay engine and was traveling at such a high rate of speed that the engine overturned less than two miles from the mill. A witness to the accident, Joan Rathbone Wilson, recalls that the train was going so fast the friction between rails and wheels sounded like music, and when the train overturned, steam rose hundreds of feet above the tall pine trees.

"Darty was killed instantly, and the company doctor, Dr. Smith, and another engineer, Mr. Corbin, who had gone along for the ride, were badly burned by the steam.

"Darty's body was placed in the back of the barber shop where it remained while attempts were made to contact relatives in Pennsylvania. He was finally buried on Graveyard Hill, but his brother arrived by train that same night with a steel casket and Darty's body was removed from the grave the next morning. His grave site was used to bury one of the foreign workers who had died on the mountain."

The iron trestle accross the Toe River at Kona carries the Yancey Railroad to join the Clinchfield main line.

13892

And, as the Common Times goes on to tell us, a song was subsequently written by Joel Robertson, a 22 year old native of Pensacola. In "The Ballad of Paul Darty", which has been sung in the hills since, Robertson tells the story of the legendary wreck.

Jean Cannon and his wife Georgia (she is also a native of South Carolina) share their love of railroading and when they speak, either of them, it is with tremendous enthusiasm. Twelve to fourteen hour days lie behind Jean Cannon's efforts to rejuvenate the Yancey Railroad, but one project that both Georgia and Jean have spent hours of time on is the rebuilding and refurbishing of the little red caboose, The Tallulah-Yancey. Always a bright spot on the line, and the delight of all the passengers on the excursion trains, Tallulah-Yancey belongs equally to Jean and Georgia. The Tallulah-Yancey is historic, having been made by hand in Cornelia, Georgia, around 1900 and put in service on the Tallulah Falls Railroad from Cornelia to Franklin, North Carolina. The little caboose worked on the Tallulah Falls line until the railroad was sold off for junk.

When the Tallulah Falls Railway went under. Jean's brother, William S. Cannon, a lifelong railroad enthusiast, went to Cornelia and purchased the caboose for Clinton Mills, Inc. The caboose stayed in Clinton on a track Bill Cannon built and was used as a on a track Bill Cannon built and was used as a Boy Scout meeting room for 14 years. The vandals took their toll, however, and Clinton Mills President, Robert Vance gave the little caboose to Bill. Having no place to put it, he offered it to Jean — who took the gift. As Bill Cannon watched one rainy night in 1974, the caboose left from Clinton on the Columbia, Newberry and Laurens Train No. 567, going north.

With the general complications of such moves, the wheel structures had been dismantled, the caboose had been put on a flatbed rail car and shipped north onto the Clinchfield and into Kona where it was reassembled back onto its own wheels. Now the Tallulah-Yancey Caboose X-5 has a brilliant red coat of paint and has been refurbished into a camper-sleeper for the Cannon family. The famous little Caboose is a favorite of everyone along the line and the Cannons frequently on warm summer evenings go picnicing along the sparkling streams — by train, of course. With Tallulah-Yancey along, the chill of the mountain air at night, is never a problem.

Considering the fate of most mountain shortlines, the Yancey Railroad, under the guidance of Jean Cannon and the others, is doing well. Like the Yancey County Common Times says: "The Yancey Railroad is here to stay."

Opposite page: The first Kenilworth Inn at Asheville.

ALEXANDER RAILROAD

As there is a legend behind every colorful appelation so is there a story behind the famous little "June Bug" line that runs between Taylorsville and Statesville, North Carolina. Now officially termed the Alexander Railroad, this hard working operation was first established in 1887 when it came together as the Statesville and Western Railroad. It was envisioned as a link between Charlotte and Tennessee and hailed as the greatest advancement in western trade for the region. The greater dreams for the proposed western link, never materialized, but with both good and bad times financially, the little Statesville and Western ran faithfully up and down its 18 mile track for a number of years.

The track was a lifeline from the little village of Taylorsville in Alexander County, and great expectations abounded for the railroad when the extremely rare and precious gem Hiddenite was discovered not far from the town, thus, the legend, and the name "June Bug". Shortly after the gem was discovered with national and international gem mining interests coming into town, a local attorney Rommulus Linney, with great excitement declared the area was so prosperous, "even a June bug could fly away with a fortune on its wing." Prosperity never quite materialized, but the train quickly became known by the "June Bug" name.

In the late 1800's, the Statesville and Western line was absorbed by another railroad company and that firm was eventually taken over by the Southern Railway System. Southern continued to operate the "June Bug" into the depression years of the 1930's. It was in 1945, that Southern announced that it was closing down the "June Bug" operations. The citizens of Taylorsville were upset by the announced closing and came together to determine what could be done to save the line. Hugh Mitchell a lawyer, found a contract which stated that Southern had to continue to operate until a solution could be found. (The Interstate Commerce Commission approved the application of Southern Railway System to abandon the branch line while World War II was still in progress. They stipulated, however, that Southern Railway could not carry out the abandonment order until the peace treaty was signed ending the war. When Southern started to abandon the line, the war had ended but a peace treaty had not been signed. Mitchell used this technicality as a way to get Southern to continue operating the branch a bit longer while local people got organized.) The Rotarians of Taylorsville with Major J. Ray Jennings, also a lawyer, called a train meeting where $20,000 toward a purchase price of $100,000 was pledged by the townsfolk that night. But soon opposition developed by those who thought the railroad "two streaks of rust, three station houses and a few tools" and the saving of it, pure folly.

It seemed then that the town would lose the train. A last ditch effort on the last day of scheduled operation, November 30, 1945, resulted in a notable response from the area industrialists, among them Julius Abernathy, and the money was raised. Shortly before the Southern crews were to begin their wrecking operations, Mayor Jennings notified Southern officials that the purchase would take place.

Lawrence P. Zachary, a salesman for a Chicago publishing house was asked to manage the line. Zachary was reluctant, but when persuaded by friends, he agreed to try it and moved into the cramped, dusty office. Zachary called on Southern for assistance and they rented him a locomotive and loaned him a few men to train his first employees, a farmer, an auto mechanic, a G.I., and a truck driver.

Zachary's first and most important chore was to get business. He went up and down the line calling on all potential customers and some that were unlikely as well. Fortunately, most had invested in the railroad and were anxious to see it succeed, they became customers and helped secure others. Within two months the train was back on a regular schedule, the first run under the new operation was on February 7, 1946. People lined the rails to see the train moving and to cheer it on. The line was re-named the Alexander Railroad. The rented locomotive from Southern was soon replaced by the line's own 45 ton General Electric diesel engine.

An article written by Nancy Alexander for the Charlotte Observer in 1968 describes how Sam Zachary, son of Lawrence, became manager of the "June Bug":

"Sam, as a youth, often rode the train with members of the crew. He graduated from Auburn and went to New York City where he was associated with American Telephone and Telegraph Company. But he never got railroading out of his system. Vacations found him back riding the line for fun.

"One day in 1952 his father telephoned him, 'Sam, how about coming home and being engineer of the railroad? We're growing and we can use you here!'

" 'I was never so glad to hear anything', recalls Sam. 'It seemed like a dream come true. Of course the salary isn't what it would be in New York, but then it doesn't take as much to live here. And I wanted my children to grow up in a small town and know the pleasures like I did'.

Sam Zachary (third from left) of the Alexander Railroad', with his crew, Eubart Flowers, brakeman; Oscar Kuykendall, Engineer; Eddie McDuffie, Conductor.

Opposite page: A heavy Shay locomotive at work in the early lumbering operations of lands now in the Pisgah National Forest.

Close up of the coupling of Engine No. 6, of the 99 ton diesel workhorse of the Alexander Railroad.

"When the elder Zachary died in 1956 the Board immediately chose Sam as manager. The formerly empty fields are now flourishing with mushrooming businesses."

The Observer article quotes Sam Zachary, "Our tracks may not be as long as some railroads but they're just as wide." A statement that gives us a clue to the engaging personality and devotion to "June Bug" of Zachary who frequently takes the train on a Sunday "day-off" run with a crew of his three children and his dog.

The present daily schedule (weekdays) is flexible, with the train making frequent stops to pick up the freight cars, along the route, the train then proceeds to Statesville to connect with the Southern main line. At present, there is no passenger service, although local residents sometimes ride up front with the engineer.

The usual speed on the line of the trim, little engine painted in the "June Bug" colors of green and gold, is 25 miles per hour, but with a heavy load, the little engine slows to six miles and sometimes as low as two miles per hour up the steep grades into Hiddenite.

The company is well housed in a remodeled, attractive building in the town of Taylorsville. Sam Zachary continues to lead his company with a flare. It is obvious he loves railroading and is a dedicated man. The Alexander Railroad is definitely as asset to the community and a service badly needed by this growing industrial region in North Carolina. But the Alexander has another highly valued asset and that is the increasing profits that Sam Zachary cites from year to year in his annual reports. The little green and gold "Junebug" may not be carrying out the "fortune" talked about by Linney, but it is a definite and desirable part of the economy of Alexander County in North Carolina.

THE ABINGDON BRANCH

The people of the Southern Mountains loved their railroads. The shining rails were a link to the outside — the world. The mountain people did not desire to live in that world, in fact, they choose not to. They chose their independence, their small farms, hillsides and vallies. Some running water, a river or a stream to sing a melodious and ever changing song. They choose to live in a house often passed from generation to generation, built by the hands of their pioneer ancestors.

But the railroads brought in the city goods, precious things like bright cloths, pottery, a new "looking glass", a set of bed springs. The railway brought the news, some of it good, some bad, but all to be talked and wondered over. And the railroad took out their farm goods.

It was like this in 1887 when the Abingdon Coal and Iron Railroad was chartered to operate to any point in North Carolina or Tennessee. An article written in May of 1976, for the Plow, a publication of Appalachian Information, Inc. by Robert S. Jones, states "Railroad Grade Road, from Todd through Brownwood and Fleetwood follows the winding South Fork of New River on the bed where steam locomotives from Abingdon, Virginia once puffed their way around mountain curves. This drive through Ashe County is perhaps along the most beautiful and scenic portion of the New River."

(Dr. Jones is a professor at Appalachian State University who has been interested in railroads all his life. The author is grateful to Dr. Jones for his permission to use material from his article.)

The construction of the new railway line began the same year as the organization of the company in Abingdon and was extended southward toward Damascus. As so often with the young railroad companies, the building soon ceased and remained at a standstill until 1900 when the company was reorganized as the Virginia-Carolina Railroad and the 16 mile stretch was completed to Damascus. In 1905, there was a total of 28 miles reaching into Konnarock. The already established Norfolk and Western Railroad bought fifty percent of the interest in the Virginia-Carolina Railroad in 1911 and the line was extended into Creek Junction, Virginia. Already the line was beginning to prosper from the rich timber lands through which it passed. In 1914, the line reached Elkland, North Carolina (now Todd), was 75 miles long over 108 bridges and had achieved the highest peak by a railroad east of the Rockies as it passed over White Top Mountain at 3,577 feet.

Elkland became a small "boom" town with a bank, a number of stores and two hotels. Norfolk and Western acquired the remaining fifty percent interest in 1917, but the line continued to operate under the Virginia-Carolina name. In 1918 it was officially designated as the Abingdon Branch of Norfolk and Western.

The "Great Flood" of 1916 did considerable damage to the railroad with the company having difficulty in recovering. In 1933 train service between West Jefferson and Elkland was discontinued.

As the mountainsides were logged over, as the roads came in and the mountain people brought in automobiles, here, as elsewhere, passenger service fell sharply.

The big trucks began to haul the freight. In 1957, the last steam powered locomotive, the Virginia Creeper, was removed from service and in 1964 all passenger service discontinued except the summer excursion trains that have run in recent years.

The parent company of Norfolk and Western petitioned the Interstate Commerce Commission in 1973 to completely abandon the Abingdon Branch. The hearings still continue. Dr. Jones in his article states that he feels 1977 will, perhaps, be the last year the railroad will operate. We think the last paragraph of his poignant article is particularly appropriate and we appreciate his permission to quote it:

"Albert Cooper (who lives in a beautiful farm house on a hill above New River) reminiscing about the past, said: 'When they took the steam engine off, the romance of railroading was gone'. Indeed, when the Abingdon Branch no longer operates, a romantic period of railroading in the Appalachian Region will come to an end."

Top: Bridge over the Big Horse Creek on the Abingdon Branch. (Note construction.)

Bottom: The architecturally beautiful station house at Abingdon, Virginia.

TWEETSIE

If ever a railroad was owned by the people it served, that railroad was the East Tennessee and Western North Carolina, with sixty-six miles of track and the homey affectionate title of "Tweetsie".

At the height of its operation, Tweetsie ran from Johnson City, Tennessee to Boone, North Carolina and it was the plaintive tone of the whistle in the mountains that earned for this spunky little train the title of "Tweetsie".

The train moved over the track in 1881 (at that time, the line reached only as far as Cranberry). Tweetsie was not one train, but many on the line, and the railroad was a thriving enterprise with many tons of freight and many passengers.

Tweetsie did a lot. She carried and dispensed many items of trade to the mountain territory, such as cloth, thread, household goods, even hardware and furniture items. The stops for passengers were sometimes a "wave down" along the tracks by a farmer headed for town.

Tweetsie was a great gossip media and spread the news of the hour and the day, passenger to passenger and out in to the communities. The route of the train was through gaps, across high trestles, along the ridges and through numerous tunnels. It was always an exciting ride.

The Cranberry Coal and Iron Company closed in 1929, leaving only the mail, some logging work and passengers, who, in increasing numbers, purchased automobiles.

This led to the fall off of business, but there were the rains of 1940 which virtually wiped out track for miles in the western part of the state. Tweetsie tried to operate on the Johnson City, Tennessee to Boone line, but continued to suffer great financial losses.

In the winter of 1940 the owners applied for and received permission to tear up the damaged track and discontinue all operations. Tweetsie, not without many protests, closed down. All rolling stock was dispersed to long-forgotten side tracks. During the second World War, the Army took two of the five remaining engines and shipped them to Alsaka where they helped build the Alcan Highway. Later the two Alaska engines were lost forever in disasters, fires, experienced by the White Pass and Yukon Railroad.

Meanwhile, Tweetsie, at home, enjoyed a revival serving the rayon plants at Elizabethton and the mountain homes of workers from around Elk Park. In July of 1950, the ET&WNC disbanded and little narrow gauge, Tweetsie, was due to pass out of the scene, or so it seemed.

No, not quite, had Tweetsie died. A group of men in Virginia bought out from ET&WNC one 460 locomotive (No. 12), one coach (No. 15) and one observation car (No. 11). The equipment was moved with great effort to a mile-long oval tract near Harrisonburg, Virginia. (A short branch of the ET&WNC continues to operate out of Johnson City, Tennessee.) Again, nature went on a rampage and Hurricane Hazel washed away much of the roadbed at Harrisonburg.

Hollywood star Gene Autrey heard about the colorful train and purchased it to ship to California. But before these plans had been carried out, the late Grover C. Robbins, Jr., of Blowing Rock and Lenoir, North Carolina saw a vision and a way to bring the little train back home. Robbins hurried to Virginia and bought out Autrey's option.

In May of 1956, Tweetsie came back to North Carolina. She was stationed in the train yards at Hickory to be overhauled. Southern could handle Tweetsie into the Hickory yard with no difficulties; it was the move from Hickory to Blowing Rock, 40 miles in length with an elevation climb of 3,800 feet over U. S. Highway 321 that would try men's souls. L. Bragg McLeod, President of Moss Trucking Company of Charlotte, young, imaginative and rising to the challenge, ventured forth to do the job.

On May 23, 1957, McLeod, at the wheel of the lead truck upon which the locomotive had been hoisted with much effort, gave the go-ahead signal and the caravan, heavily loaded, began the climb up the mountain at daybreak. Accompanying the labor trucks were Spencer Percival and Frank Coffee of the Carolina and Northwestern Railroad, a part of the Southern Railway System. Also along were telephone and power helpers and a mobile unit from a local radio station. People by the hundreds lined the route and the caravan stopped briefly in Lenoir before tackling the roughest, most uphill part of the journey.

Tweetsie's new tracks had been laid on a beautiful high hill halfway between Boone and Blowing Rock. The approach was steep and freshly graded. Two bulldozers, one pushing and one pulling, took the units, one by one, to the summit and onto the track. When the last unit was firmly in place, a sigh went up from the crowd. It had been a long day, a big day, a day of much excitement.

Tweetsie was in the full glory of lustrous brass and "Tweetsie Railway" was painted on the cab in shining gold.

Tweetsie was now a fancy lady who would broadcast the famous Tweetsie call through the mountains of North Carolina, and children and grownups were to come by the hundreds to ride the jaunty little steamer.

They still do.

"Tweetsie" the old ET & WNC, comes up the mountain by truck to rest on a circle track on a mountain between Boone and Blowing Rock, North Carolina.

CLINCHFIELD RAILROAD

As the modern day, heavy diesels of the Clinchfield polish up the rails between Spartanburg, South Carolina and the northern terminus of Elkhorn City in Kentucky, they are rolling over miles of historic land.

It is within this territory, that Daniel Boone lived, fought and explored. It was in March of 1775 that Boone, who had gathered together a group of 30 frontier axemen and oxen, began to cut a trail from upper Virginia, through the Powel River valley, across the Cumberland Mountains into Central Kentucky. The rocky, mountainous route became known as the Wilderness Road and for long years was the only passage into the rich farm land of Kentucky. By 1800, it was estimated that more than 200,000 settlers had traveled the route.

This is also the land of the lesser known John Sevier, "Nolichucky Jack", who in a move years ahead of its time, 1772, established the Watauga Association, a group of settlers along the Watauga River between the unsettled boundaries of North Carolina and Virginia, who declared themselves and their land holdings free and clear of English domination, and established the State of Franklin, the first men of American birth to create an independent government on the North American Continent. It was only natural then that Sevier was elected the first governor of the new, independent state. In 1780, he led a force of troops in an arduous trek over the Great Smokies to aid in the defeat of the British at Kings Mountain. With the war won, and his term as governor over, North Carolina endeavored to resume authority over Franklin, moving to impound Sevier's possessions and slaves and removing them to the house of a man named Tipton near where Sinking Creek crosses the route of the Clinchfield. Sevier gathered a group of his friends and marched against the North Carolina Militia on Tipton's farm. A battle raged, between the two forces up and down the present route of the railroad. In subsequent events, the State of Franklin was absorbed into the newly formed state of Tennessee and Sevier later then became Governor of that state.

The better known stories of railroad construction west from Old Fort and north over Saluda by other railroad companies, have somewhat overshadowed the history, the tortuous building of the mighty Clinchfield.

On August 22, 1908, on the first trip over the nearly completed Clinchfield line (other than those taking company officials and construction crews) Col. Fred A. Olds, who was with the North Carolina Historical Commission in Raleigh, described it in a newspaper article as "A railway in Cloudland" and, "The Rhododendron Route".

For our story of the Clinchfield, we return to the statesman, John C. Calhoun of South Carolina and his dream in 1832 of a road from Charleston to Cincinnati. The main obstacle, as everyone recognized was the unprecedented barrier of the Blue Ridge Mountains. In the northern states, the railroad builders had found it comparatively easy to negotiate gaps and passes in the Appalachians. But the Southern dreamers of a short railway route to the midwest had to reckon with the massive height and ruggedness of the Blue Ridge, the Great Blacks, the Nantahalas, the Great Smokies, all a part of the Southern Appalachians. In 1879, the Western North Carolina Railroad crossed the Blue Ridge wall at Swannanoa Gap and for a time the push for a more direct route lay dormant.

The author shoots the back cover shot of the Yancey No. 2. Right is David Riddle of the Yancey line. The Toe River is in the back ground and above that the Clinchfield.

In 1886, General John H, Wilder, an iron capitalist of Chattanooga, Tennessee a former Union officer in the Civil War and the builder of the once popular Cloudland Hotel on Roan Mountain became interested. He assembled, that year, a group of capitalists who were willing to invest their money in a railroad to connect the rich coal fields of southwestern Virginia and eastern Kentucky with both the North and the South by a route across the mountains from some point on the Ohio River to the Atlantic Coast. The group organized the Charleston, Cincinnati and Chicago Railroad Company which was to become known as the "Three C's". The route was to be from Charleston to Marion, across the Blue Ridge to Johnson City, through Virginia to Ashland, Kentucky, a distance of 621 miles. The Company surveyed the entire route and succeeded in completing two sections, one south from Marion to Kingville, South Carolina and the other south from Johnson City to Chestoa, Tennessee. General Wilder and the company had interested English capitalists and up to that time approximately $7,000,000 in British monies had been spent. In 1893, however, the failure of Baring Brothers, the English Bankers, forced suspension of work and the company was thrown into the throes of foreclosure proceedings. Under this threat the railroad was purchased by Charles E. Hellier, who then organized, in 1894, a new corporation, The Ohio River and Charleston Railway Company. In 1899 the new company extended the line 20 miles from Chestoa to five miles south of Huntdale, North Carolina.

In 1902, a new president was elected, Col. George L. Carter, and under his bold direction, the group geared themselves to complete the route. Carter was cited in newspaper articles as "The father of the

revised plan of modern railroad of low grades
and easy curvature to connect the Ohio Valley
with the Atlantic Coastal Plain."
And the sentence doesn't say it, doesn't
ever hint at the tremendous amount of human
endeavor that was to be expended on such a
project. Nor does it mention the untold loss of
lives. Lives that were to be taken, uncounted,
unrecorded, buried in hastily dug graves along
the sides of the road bed.

Carter and his associates purchased the right
of way and reformed the company into the
South and Western Railway. They bought up
large tracts of the now famous Clinchfield
coal region, known then as the "Clinchfield
Section". The line was soon completed to
Spruce Pine and rapidly became a
tremendous aid to the economy of that whole
section of North Carolina, rich in minerals and
lumber. But here at Spruce Pine the work
halted.

Possibly the hesitation was caused due to a
shortage of funds. We know the company was,
once again, reorganized and came under the
direction of John B. Dennis, a man who felt
a great need to further the work on the
railroad. He wanted to increase the industrial
development of the territory. We think,
though, that the temporary pause was for the
company to gather its forces together morally,
physically, and financially in order to attack
what still stands today as one of the most
trying and difficult building jobs in the history
of railroading. It also was to be one of the most
costly, both in lives and money. In 1905, with
an army of crews, supervisors, mules and
crude equipment assembled, work began. Not
only did the tough and rugged men almost
literally throw themselves against the
mountains as they penetrated the steep and
boulder strewn slopes, they daily battled each
other.

81

*Opposite page: From an old post card, Toxaway Inn
in the Sapphire Country of North Carolina.*

*Old abandoned caboose of the Abingdon Branch
at Todd.*

From an old clipping from the Charlotte Observer, written in 1953 by Ashton Chapman, of Spruce Pine, we can draw together the story. This was remote backwoods country, miles out to civilization sometimes without a footpath, and as Chapman relates: "Italians, Germans and Russians were recruited in northern cities, many were just off boats in New York. Few had little, if any knowledge of English. The construction company had to employ an interpreter who was kept busy going up and down the line from one to another of the labor camps to help settle disputes and explain various matters to the immigrants. Some native labor was also employed and a number of Negroes were brought in.

"These construction years were the most turbulent this area has ever known. With such an admixture of racial background and temperaments, with the laborers, crowded into tiny tar-paper shacks lining the muddy, rocky camp 'streets' anything could happen and often did. Innumerable fights and sometimes murder were natural results."

Chapman goes on to tell of one group of 15 Italians who, disdaining the ordinary back country fare, had hired their own cook. Coming home one evening, the group discovered him drunk and no supper fixed, not for the first time by any means. Apparently this was the last straw. They sobered him up, summarily held a trial and pronounced the cook guilty. The sentence, according to their own laws was that he be tied to a tree and shot. According to the story, the sentence was promptly executed. But later the Italians were taken to Raleigh and stood trial themselves — for murder, with four or five of them sentenced to prison terms of from five to ten years.

One of the roughest of all the camps on the Clinchfield was number four, with a record of hard fighting men, drunkenness, rowdyness and crime that defies description. In 1907, a new superintendent, Captain Felix Kidd from Harlan, Kentucky was brought in and the word was whispered throughout the camp that "Kidd's little, but he's loud and he covers every inch of ground he stands on!" While Kidd seemingly didn't know the meaning of fear, he also became a challenge to the rough citizens of the camp, to soon boil down to a direct duel between Jim Anderson, a cold-blooded, reckless gang-boss, tougher than the toughest but of long experience in building railroads.

Anderson in a drunken ruckus one Sunday afternoon disobeyed almost all of Kidd's orders for peace keeping in the camp. Kidd, cool-headed and calm with his pistol on his hip fired Anderson who quit, but wouldn't leave camp. He went to his brother Will's shack and continued to drink and raise a commotion where upon Kidd, again with his gun at the ready, called the two brothers out. Kidd, backed up by two of his deputies, Bert Horne, the construction company's time keeper and Charley Hale, a young boy whom Kidd had befriended and given a job, called the Andersons out and the five of them marched down the hill to the company office where Kidd intended to have Horne pay the two brothers off and then the group would escort them out of the camp.

Suddenly, as the five men crowded into the door of the pay shack, wild pushing and flailing broke out. There ensued gun shots, some behind the door of the shack which had banged to on Horne, Jim Anderson, Kidd and Hale. When the shooting ceased, Anderson and Kidd were dead. Horne freely admitted that at the first shot he had dived

Opposite page: In 1896, a big steamer pulls into the Salisbury, North Carolina Station. Please note "Southern" on the side. The Southern Railroad Company had been organized two years before.

1398
1388

Langren Hotel, Asheville, N. C.
Completed 1912. Fire Proof. Constructed of concrete, steel,
iron and sandstone.

under the desk and consequently, in trying to dodge bullets, didn't see a thing. In a trial that rocked the whole community, young Hale, under 20 years old and who obviously had shot Jim Anderson in defense of his mentor, Kidd (his bullet was the one that killed Anderson) was brought to Marion and tried for murder. Most everyone in the county knew he was framed and when he was pronounced guilty of murder in the second degree and sentenced to ten years at hard labor in the State Penitentiary, there was an uproar from the citizenry, but to no avail. After serving two years of his term, young Hale escaped and was never caught or heard from again.

If the murders, the rum and cocaine running, the thieving and carousing were bad, the accidents were if anything, worse.

Reid Queen, Sr., who was Little Switzerland's first postmaster and who worked as a pipefitter on the miles of steam lines supplying power to drill the holes for the tons of dynamite required to blast the rock was 72 years of age when, in 1953, he told a story of how one day a large gang was struggling to excavate some mud and loose rock at the base of a thirty foot cut when the upper part of the bank suddenly caved in burying seven of the men under tons of dirt. All were from the Bear Creek section of Mitchell County and all died.

That same day, as Queen told Chapman, nine more workers were killed in Upper Bridle Path Tunnel by an explosion. Some 15 cases, containing 100 pounds of dynamite each, had been stored in the tunnel. A careless worker, was using a sharp stone to break open the heavy wooden dynamite boxes, when suddenly the whole mountain was rocked by a thunderous blast. While those outside waited fearfully, the smoke, fumes and dust settled and when they entered they were able to recover only three of the bodies. "Remains of the other six were splattered all over the rocky walls of the tunnel."

In a bloodthirsty riot at camp six, led by a man named Jimmy Mazone, five were killed and "buried under the chestnut tree by the Honeycutt Tunnel, all being in a row." There were other riots, accidents and the death toll continued to mount until the road made its way through the Blue Ridge to Marion and the first trains came in in 1908. The first passenger train entered Spartanburg, Southern terminus of the Clinchfield in 1909.

The road had followed in general, the old route of the "Three C's", but with new surveys for low grades and easy curves. In 1908, the name had been changed to the Carolina, Clinchfield and Ohio Railway Company (The Clinchfield coming from the Clinch River).

In all, there are 54 tunnels on the Clinchfield. In the last, most desperate struggle of construction, as one travels north from Marion the 17 tunnels are Honeycutt, 1688 feet; Fourth Rocky, 179; Third Rocky, 420; Second Rocky, 757; First Rocky, 716; Byrd, 341; Lower Pine, 2211; Speedy, 288; Lower Bridle, 1618; Snipes, 637; Third Washburn, 915; Quinn's Knob, 545; Second Washburn, 363; First Washburn, 770; Upper Bridle, 927; Upper Pine, 1600; Blue Ridge, 1865. (The longest tunnel on the Clinchfield is the Sandy Ridge between Trammel and Dante, Virginia at 7854 feet.) North of Spruce Pine there is Vance Tunnel at 527 feet and further north, Brush Creek Tunnel, 304 feet. South of Marion is the Marion Tunnel which is 1,073 feet. In all, the last 20 miles of the Clinchfield between Spruce Pine and Marion was probably more costly in lives and money than any other railroad in the south. There is no record

Opposite page: The Langren Hotel, located on the corner across from the present day Northwestern Bank building in Asheville, North Carolina.

of the loss of lives, but the construction costs on this section ran better than $1,000,000 per mile.

With its 54 tunnels, the Clinchfield was 3.5 per cent of its total length underground, more than any other railroad in America today.

This final stretch of the Clinchfield, from Marion to Altapass, the train climbs 1,313 feet in 31.5 miles. To accomplish this, the roadbed is constructed in a magnificent loop system consisting of a series of seven stages winding around the valleys, climbing in a long developing curve. Below the Blue Ridge Tunnel the road makes a seven mile loop through nine tunnels to ascend approximately 300 feet in elevation. At another point, the direct line to a corresponding point on the upper grade is some 300 feet while the rail distance is over two miles. On a clear day, in the fall, after the leaves have gone, one can stand at the mouth of the Blue Ridge Tunnel, and count 14 different views of a train as it travels the loop.

No railroad had been built, up to this time, that had overcome the difficulties the Clinchfield had faced.

Late in 1924, the Atlantic Coastline Railroad Company and the Louisville and Nashville Railroad Company leased the properties of the Carolina, Clinchfield and Ohio for a period of 999 years and from this merging of interests came the present name of the company when the operations of the newly formed Clinchfield Railroad Company began on December 1, 1925. Today, the Clinchfield operates daily over the line. Like most of the other railroads, with the coming of the automobile and the building of good highways, the Clinchfield has lost its passenger service, but it remains a thriving, profit making operation, now under the general

management of Thomas D. Moore, Jr., (he also holds the title of Executive Vice President). It is under his leadership that the railroad has grown and thrived into its present healthy financial condition. Moore, a native of South Carolina, began his railroad career with Southern Railway in their Engineering and Maintenance of Way Department, then as Trainmaster, and a Superintendent of four of their division. He joined the Seaboard Coastline, serving as Superintendent on two divisions and then was promoted to Assistant to Operating Vice President in 1966, then to General Manager of the Clinchfield on June 1, 1968.

Moore has been very active in civic and community affairs in the region, serving on numerous business and social service boards.

It was Moore who was responsible for resurrecting the old Clinchfield Number 1, a tiny steamer 95 years old, that had been abandoned in the Clinchfield yards. When Moore saw the rusty wreck which had been cast off from service in 1955, and heard the stories about how the locomotive had pulled the first relief trains into Johnstown, Pennsylvania after the great flood of 1889. He set a swarm of sheet metal craftsmen to work on the Clinchfield, Number 1 "Spot" as the engine was called, and in a seven weeks around the clock effort, the restoration job was complete. Then power became the problem. So with an ingenious touch, the railroaders disguised two diesels into old style Pullman cars and hooked them up into a Hostler's control operation inside the cab. With the new power, the little engine could pull a heavy load of cars. The Clinchfield Number 1 now operates on the line as an excursion engine and to haul the yearly "Santa Claus Special."

It is on Saturday after Thanksgiving, at exactly

10:00 a.m. that the biggest event of the year for many families along the northern 93 miles of the Clinchfield begins to happen. The "Santa Claus Special" with Ed Hatcher, engineer at throttle, his brother George Hatcher, at the firebox and Tom Moore in his private car pulls out from Elkhorn City, Kentucky and heads south. On board are thousands of gifts, clothing and candy. Santa himself, (John Dudney, Kingsport postmaster in real life) reigns from the back car and employees of the railroad distribute the goodies to some 25,000 children of the coal mining section of the Appalachian region, who gather along the route. The yearly event is co-sponsored by the Kingsport Chamber of Commerce and the Clinchfield Railroad.

Down through the years, through the constant upgrading of equipment, the coming of the diesels and up-to-date signal systems, there has been hardly any modification of route or rails other than necessary general repairs.

The Clinchfield serves us today as the next advancing step in engineering concepts that were developed after the first epic struggles of railroad building that took place in these mountains west from Old Fort and over Saluda.

These concepts served those who later went out to crisscross other mountain ranges with "high iron". The long loops, tunnels, trestles deep cuts of the Clinchfield are an enduring engineering wonder and those who have daring work of this nature to accomplish in today's world come to ride this train and wonder at it.

We come to the end as we always do, a time when the facts as we know them are marshalled into what we hope is readable and interesting material. Already, we are looking back over the "times" of the book, the many wonderful experiences, the rides we were permitted to take on the trains, old and new, the pictures we were given — those taken from old albums, dug from old trunks, the eager scanning of worn and scratched negatives, to be printed with care and patience. And already now we are looking back and dreaming again with the "old timers," an expression that has nothing at all to do with age but with people who have had a part in the shaping of a certain time, a certain place, a series of events and who will remember for us. Those who will return with us to another year, another hour, and will share, so that memories can be preserved for some future time .

The "old timers" have given us their gifts, their priceless gifts of memory, and we thank them.

They talk to us in a way far more graphic than any old clipping, book or picture.

They recall, these "old timers" of the railroad, the settling in of a long run, how it is to pull the iron cloak of power and speed around you — to make the rhythm of the whole thing work, the fireman with his pitched stroke at the blazing firebox, the clacky-clack of the wheels turning — turning — turning — beating the minutes and the hours away, far into the night.

They remember how it feels to be a trainman, the liquid blackness of a rainy night, the icy wind from a snowy mountain, sweat running in the heat of a summer day and the falling dew of a foggy morning.

And the sounds, they remember the sounds, the clash of gigantic gears, the sudden deafening blow of steam, the abbreviated call of the conductor. Then like giant hammers, the pistons crashing down, the clang of the huge cars, one against the other as they began to move.

Out on the rails and rolling, they remember the big wheels pounding like a heartbeat, magnified a million times and racing three hundred strokes a minute. Once again, the world is theirs.

They share with us, the old timers, and it is then, only then, that the long, low whistle comes calling, clear and sweet along the river of remembrance, echoing back to us from the hillside, down through the valley of time.

The first Battery Park Hotel at Asheville.

IMPORTANT DATES

1767
The first iron rails to carry a moving vehicle made by an iron works of England.

1769
The first steam engine patented by James Watt of Scotland.

1804
The first steam railway locomotive built by Richard Trevithick of England.

1814
The first train of cars pulled by George Stephenson's locomotive in England.

1825
Stockton and Darlington of England run the first regularly operated steam railroad.

1825
John Stevens builds the first locomotive to run on rails in the United States, at Hoboken, New Jersey.

1830
The locomotive, Best Friend of Charleston, begins the first regularly scheduled railway run in the United States, from Charleston, South Carolina to Hamburg (now a part of the Southern Railway System).

1830
First locomotive to burn coal, The Tom Thumb built by Peter Cooper and begins operation out of Baltimore, Maryland.

1831
The South Carolina Railroad begins the first railway mail service out of Charleston.

1831
The locomotive cowcatcher invented by Isaac Dripps of Camden and Amboy Railroad in New Jersey.

1832
John C. Calhoun of South Carolina, proposes a railroad over the Blue Ridge Mountains into the mid-west.

1833
Andrew Jackson becomes the first President to take a ride on a railroad.

1837
The world's first sleeping car put on the run between Harrisburg and Chambersburg, Pennsylvania.

1850
Start in organization of the Blue Ridge Railroad, late to become known as Tallulah Falls Railroad.

1851
The telegraph first used in directing trains. (Erie Railroad)

1852
The first survey of the North Carolina Railroad over the Blue Ridge Mountains into Western North Carolina is made.

1856
Construction of the North Carolina Railroad into the mountains is begun.

1858
Regularly scheduled runs are made from Salisbury to Statesville, North Carolina.

1859
First Pullman built sleeping car is put on line between Bloomington and Chicago, Illinois.

1861
Outbreak of the Civil War in the United States, thus begins first "railroad war" in which mass troops are moved on rails by steam locomotives.

1863
The first railway dining cars are put on the run between Baltimore and Philadelphia.

(Note: The dates listed are not intended as a complete historical record of railroading. Some listed are national, some of the Southern Appalachian region. The selection was made at random by the author solely for the general interest of the reader.)

On a grant from the Appalachian Consortium, Danny Phillipps, a history student at Mars Hill College, traveled north to locate this climax engine in Ann Arbor, Michigan. The search was a part of his work-study program for the college. The engine was one that had been used first by the Champion Paper and Fibre Company, then by the Bemis Lumber Company in logging operations in the southern mountains. It has been restored as a part of the U. S. Forest Service Cradle of Forestry near Brevard, North Carolina and is now operating on a track there. Shown with the locomotive are: (left to right) Dr. Harley Jolley, Professor, Mars Hill College; William R. Sweet, Landscape Architect, U. S. Forest Service; John R. McGuire, Chief, U. S. Forest Service; Robert W. Cermak, Forest Supervisor, National Forests in N. C.; and James Reid, District Ranger, Pisgah Ranger District.

1869
The first trans-Continental railway completed with a golden spike being driven at Promotory Point in Utah.

1877
First locomotive on rails, in steam, arrives in Tryon, North Carolina over the Spartanburg-Asheville Railroad.

1879
The Swannanoa Tunnel opened on the Western North Carolina Railroad.

1879
First engine, on rails, in steam, arrives at Hendersonville, North Carolina over the Spartanburg-Asheville Railroad.

1880
The first engine, in steam, on rails, arrives at Asheville, North Carolina.

1882
The westward route of the Western North Carolina Railroad completed to Paint Rock from Asheville.

1883
The Standard Time System, sponsored by the railroads is adopted throughout the nation.

1885
Round Knob Hotel at Andrews Geyser on the Western North Carolina Railroad built by Major James W. Wilson.

1886
First Battery Park Hotel, built by Col. Frank Coxe opened.

1887
The Charleston, Cincinnati and Chicago Railway organized by John H. Wilder of Chattanooga, Tennessee (later to become the Clinchfield Railroad).

1889
Asheville-Spartanburg Railway completed from Hendersonville into Asheville, North Carolina.

1889
Street cars began running in Asheville (reputed to be the second such system in the country).

1890
Route of Western North Carolina Railroad completed from Asheville to Murphy to become known as "The Murphy Branch".

1890
Beginning of the first big building "boom" in Western North Carolina.

1892 (Approximately)
Railroad built to the site of Biltmore House and construction begins on the mansion.

1893
Locomotive Number 999 makes world's first 100 mile per hour run.

1894
Last river drive of lumber from the Snowbird Mountains into Chattanooga, Tennessee.

1894
The Southern Railway is organized under a special act of the Virginia Legislature.

1895
First successful electric locomotive is put on a regular run by Baltimore & Ohio.

1903
Round Knob Hotel burns.

1903
Toxaway Inn opens in the Sapphire Valley region of Western North Carolina.

1904
The Tallulah Falls Railroad complete to Clayton, Georgia.

1905

The Southern Railway formally assumes operation of the old Western North Carolina Railroad.

1905

Incorporation, by special act of the General Assembly of North Carolina of the Graham County Railroad.

1907

Tallulah Falls Railroad completed to Franklin, North Carolina.

1908

The Clinchfield Railroad completed into Marion, North Carolina.

1909

First passenger train enters Spartanburg, South Carolina on the Clinchfield Railroad.

1909

Kenilworth Inn, owned by Joseph M. Grazzam, George W. Vanderbilt and Southern Railway burns.

1916

"The Great Flood" renders inestimable damage to the railroads of the Southern Appalachian area.

1916

Toxaway Dam destroyed by storms, Towaway Inn closed down.

1924

New Battery Park Hotel opened in Asheville.

1925

The arrival in Robbinsville, of the first locomotive on rails, in steam, over the Graham County Railroad from Topton in Western North Carolina.

1925

First diesel engine placed in service.

1937

The world's longest railroad, the Trans Siberian between Moscow, Russia and Nakhodka, China, a total of 5,800 miles completed at a cost of $500,000,000.

1945

The Alexander Railroad is opened between Taylorsville and Statesville, North Carolina.

1955

An electric locomotive makes a 200 miles per hour run for the first time, between Bordeaux and Dax, France.

1956

Alexander Railroad management and ownership assumed locally by the citizens of Alexander County in North Carolina and surrounding area. (Formerly a part of the Southern Railway.)

1956

"Tweetsie" of the old East Tennessee and Western North Carolina Railroad comes back to be established as a tourist train on a circular tract between the towns of Boone and Blowing Rock, North Carolina.

1961

Last run of the Tallulah Falls Railroad.

1966

"Bear Creek Junction" tourist railroad is established as a part of the Graham County Railroad.

1975

Two trestles on Graham County line destroyed by storm. Three months later, Graham County Railroad and Bear Creek Junction shut down.

RAILROAD NOMENCLATURE

DERAIL — 1) off the track; 2) a device to protect the main line on a side track by derailing a car or cars. (Two common types: Toad, because it sits on top of the rail; Alligator, an opening in the rail.

YARD BOARD — Yard limit sign.

COCKED SWITCH — Half thrown switch.

SPLIT SWITCH — A switch damaged by running through it the wrong way with a train.

CUT — 1) a block of cars; 2) to uncouple, make a cut.

CUT-OFF — 1) laid off due to lack of work; 2) uncouple.

EXTRA — 1) a train not in the time table; 2) to work different jobs (vacations, off sick, unassigned, etc.,) left vacant by others; 3) a stretch of track that is a by-pass.

EXTRA BOARD — The list of men working extra.

CHAIN GANG — The list of men working extra trains over a certain portion of a division. Also called pool work (Western term).

HIGH BALL — Go ahead. Take off. All clear to go.

HOGHEAD — Slang term for engineer. Derived from the use of the term "hog" for a big, slow steam locomotive. (Also, hogger or hogineer)

TALLOW POT — Old term for a fireman.

HIGHIRON — Main line.

GOAT — Switch engine.

SPOT — To place a car (or cars) in a place for loading or unloading.

SPOT, ON THE — To stand idle with nothing to do (coffee break, etc.).

BEANS — Lunch.

JOB — Any position of employment. A man may be an engineer and work several "jobs" a month. Each on a different train or switch engine. Each is called a "job". Usually assigned by number; i.e., Job #872 or #721 or #521.

BOOMER — A drifter. Working several railroads during his life.

HOMEGUARD — A person who stays in the same yard or same division all his life.

MARKER — The light at the end of train, showing red to the rear to protect the train. Also designates the train is complete.

THAT'S GOOD — Stop. A verbal command as opposed to a printed sign, etc. Also *not* an emergency command.

THAT'LL DO — Same as "That's Good."

HOLD 'EM — Stop. An emergency command. Also, plug 'em, big hole 'em.

TAG — Written or typed list of cars to be used by trainmen or switchmen, showing where to pick up, spot or set out cars, also switch list.

WIND — Air as used in air brakes.

BLEED — Drain all the air out of the brakes on a car.

BUMPER — Anything to stop a car from rolling off the end of a track.

CLOCK — Air gauge in locomotive or caboose.

DAYS — Demerits. Usually more than 90 at any time is enough to cause dismissal from service. Usually removed from personnel record on a 5 to 1 working day-demerit day basis.

LINK — A train crossing over between two parallel tracks. Also a cross-over.

BEND THE RAIL — Throw a switch. Also, bend the iron.

AGAINST THE CURRENT — Opposite direction from normal "Current of Traffic". Also, against the grain or against the breeze.

ON THE GROUND — Off the track.

PULL THE AIR — Put air brakes in emergency. Also "Dump the air", "plug 'em", "big hole", "clean the clock".

BINDER — Brakes, usually a hand brake.

CAR TOAD — Car inspector, derived from the squatting position to see under the cars. Also "Car Knocker", "Car Tink".

MUD HOP — A clerk who walks between the tracks to check the cars in a yard.

PICK-UP — To pickup cars along the way.

SET-OUT — To leave cars. Also "Set-off".

CAB — Caboose, also Hack, crummy, way car, car.

STOVE — Steam locomotive. Also lokie, western loggers term for locomotive.

CLUB — A baseball size stick to help turn brake wheel on hand brake. Also brake bat.

HOT BOX — Overheated axle bearing.

HAND BOMBER — Hand fired steam locomotive; also muzzle loader.

SNAKE — A switchman. Derived from the large "S" in the middle of their union buttons.

SAND HOUSE — 1) where sand is stored for locomotives; 2) gossip, rumors, etc., derived from sitting in the warm sand house during bad weather and talking.

BRANCH — A feeder line to the mainline. Usually light track and small trains.

DRAG — A slow, heavy, freight train.

VARNISH — Passenger train.

HOG LAW — The law limiting the number of hours, in a 24-hour period, that a man may work. Used to be 16 hours but has been cut to 12 now (1974), (Also, Dog Law).

DIE ON THE LAW — To be caught away from terminal at the end of 12 hours of work and having to leave train for another crew to take over.

DEHORN — Take away one's authority. Demote.

JOIN THE BIRDS — Jump off the train.

CORNFIELD MEET — Head-on wreck.

BEAT HER ON THE BACK — Run a locomotive fast and hard. Also, "Lay the hickory to her."

TO BULLETIN — To offer a job for bid. Also a slang expression to get rid of. "I'm going to bulletin the old lady's job if the coffee doesn't get better."

FLIMSY — A train order. So-called because it is printed on lightweight paper.

TIEUP — Go off duty at end of day.

HEAD MAN — Head brakeman. Also Headshack.

FLAGMAN — Rear brakeman. Also rear man, rear shack.

DROP — To pull cars with engine. Uncouple them, speed up the engine and run over a switch, throw switch and allow cars to go in to the other track. Object: to get cars on opposite end of engine. (Western U.S. term)

FLYING SWITCH — Same as a Drop (Eastern U.S. term). Also a "Jerk".

CURRENT — The normal direction of traffic on a multi-track main line.

HAYBURNER — Coal/oil lamp.

PULL THE PIN — To uncouple car (or cars), also to quit, resign or get rid of. (He pulled the pin on the girlfriend the other day.)

JOINT — A coupling. More correctly, to "make a joint"; also, to make a "hook".

LINE-UP — 1) to throw a switch; 2) to have all the switches thrown for a particular route; 3) a list of the trains due to arrive or depart a place. Usually for an eight-hour period. Not a timetable as a "line-up" shows extra trains, too; 4) switch cars to suit a list or order.

BRAINS — Conductor.

ACKNOWLEDGEMENTS

I am grateful to my husband Dick, who by his usual patience and encouragement made this book possible. I am grateful to my brother Kyle Morgan, who aided in many ways, listened to much, counseled a lot and helped me take and assemble the photos. I appreciate the assistance of the "old timers", Ed Collins, J. B. Waldrup, C. C. Bateman, and certainly, Howard Herd who is not an old timer, but who listened (and sometimes criticized) but encouraged and assisted throughout.

There are many to thank, Ewart M. Ball, III, who took many of the photos, William F. Geeslin and Charles O. Morgret of The Southern Railway System, Washington, D.C., who provided material and photos. I would like to acknowledge the great assistance of J. V. Cannon and his wife Georgia Young Cannon who spent hours with us in assembling and going over material and who were kind enough to aid us in our photographing of the Yancey Railroad; the many others who spent time in reviewing material, among them, Sam Zachary of the Alexander Railroad and William A. V. Cecil of Biltmore House.

My appreciation is extended to the Appalachian Consortium, Boone, N.C., for providing me with materials and assistance.

Especially, would I like to mention Betty Betz, Custodian of the North Carolina Room at Pack Memorial Library who not only saw me through this book, but previous ones as well; The Asheville Citizen-Times, which is most conscious of our great regional historical heritage and whose editor, Luther Thigpen generously allowed me to quote from the newspaper; Jody Higins who allowed me to quote from the Yancey County Times; David Lawrence, Editor of the Charlotte Observer who permitted me to quote from his paper; and The Plow News Magazine, published by Appalachian Information, Inc., Abingdon, Virginia.

Ralph Burns spent hours in the darkroom coaching printable quality from ancient negatives. Frankie Pegg, friend and typist who patiently struggled through the original manuscript and many re-writes. Bob Kelso, our designer, always refers to me in the third person, as "The Author" (especially when disapproving of something), but , as always, tried his utmost, as did his associates, to please us and we appreciate him.

Most especially are we grateful to Thomas D. Moore, Jr., General Manager of the Clinchfield Railroad, his Staff Assistant Herman Mays and the many others of the Clinchfield line who helped us so much. (See Front Cover Story)

ASHEVILLE CHAPTER, NATIONAL RAILWAY HISTORICAL SOCIETY, INC.

The Asheville Chapter of the National Railway Historical Society is a non-profit organization dedicated to the preservation of railroad history. The Chapter first met in January of 1986 and was chartered by the National Society on April 20, 1986.

The goals of the Asheville Charter are to promote an interest in railway transportation and to educate the general public about railroading and the role of railroads in the history of Western North Carolina and the United States. These goals are accomplished by Chapter sponsorship of rail trips, rail exhibits, collecting and preserving railroad historical material, and issuing publications on railroad subjects. The Chapter's long-range plans include the establishment of a railroad museum in Asheville.

During its relatively short existence, the Asheville Chapter, NRHS, has enjoyed healthy growth — from 10 members at its chartering a little over three years ago to over 100 members today. During the same time period, the Chapter has sponsored many rail excursions to such North Carolina destinations as Hickory, Statesville and Old Fort as well as trips into eastern Tennessee. Two steam locomotives have visited Asheville to power some of these trips: L & N Engine No. 152 and N & W Class 'A' articulated No. 1218.

Monthly meetings of the Asheville Chapter, NRHS, are held at the North Asheville Recreational Center, 27 E. Larchmont (off Merrimon Avenue behind First Union Bank), Asheville, North Carolina, on the third Monday of each month at 7:30 p.m. Meetings consist of a short business session followed by a program of railroading interest. Visitors are welcome at these meetings without charge.

As host for the 1989 NRHS Annual Convention, the Asheville Chapter, NRHS is sponsoring this Third Printing of **Trains, Trestles, and Tunnels — Railroads of Southern Appalachia** in the conviction that the work is in keeping with the objectives of the National Railway Historical Society.